THE Elementary DOCTRINES

THE Elementary DOCTRINES

SAM SOLEYN & NICHOLAS SOLEYN

Translated into Spanish by
Dr. Hernando Caicedo

Copyright © 2015 - by Sam Soleyn and Nicholas Soleyn

Publisher—eGenCo

All rights reserved. This book is protected by the copyright laws of the United States of America. This book may not be copied or reprinted for commercial gain or profit. The use of short quotations or occasional page copying for personal or group study is permitted and encouraged. Permission for other usages must be obtained from Soleyn Publishing LLC. Unless otherwise identified, Scripture quotations are from the HOLY BIBLE, NEW INTERNATIONAL VERSION®, copyright © 1973, 1978, 1984 and 2010 International Bible Society. Used by permission of Zondervan. All rights reserved. Scripture quotations marked NKJV are from the New King James Version. Copyright © 1982 by Thomas Nelson, Inc. Used by permission. All rights reserved. Scripture quotations marked KJV are from the King James Version. Scripture quotations taken from the New American Standard Bible®, Copyright © 1960, 1962, 1963, 1968, 1971, 1972, 1973, 1975, 1977, 1995 by The Lockman Foundation Used by permission. All emphasis within Scripture is the author's own.

SoleynPublishing LLC
Soleyn Publishing LLC
PO Box 67456, Albuquerque, NM 87193-7456, USA
www.soleynpublishing.com
contact@soleynpublishing.com
facebook.com/soleynpublishing
twitter.com/SoleynPublish

eGenCo
Generation Culture Transformation
Specializing in publishing for generation culture change

eGenCo
824 Tallow Hill Road
Chambersburg, PA 17202, USA
Phone: 717-461-3436
Email: info@egen.co
Website: www.egen.co

facebook.com/egenbooks
youtube.com/egenpub
egen.co/blog

Publisher's Cataloging-in-Publication Data
Soleyn, Sam. Nick Solelyn
The Elementary Doctrines.; by Sam Soleyn and Nick Solelyn.
176 pages cm.
ISBN: 978-1-68019-900-0 paperback
    978-1-68019-901-7 ebook
    978 1 60819 902 4 ebook
1. Religion. 2. Maturity. 3. Christian Lifestyle. I. Title
2014954554

Cover design and page layout by Kevin Lepp, www.kmlstudio.com

DEDICATION

    This book is dedicated to those who have tirelessly labored with me in spreading the message of the Kingdom of God. Among them, I wish to specifically note Doug and Nancy Allen and John and Bobby Huckabay.

Sam Soleyn

    I dedicate this book to Rebecca, Selah, and Zion.

Nick Soleyn

TABLE OF CONTENTS

	Introduction	01
Chapter One	Repentance From Acts That Lead to Death	11
Chapter Two	Faith Toward God	23
Chapter Three	Baptisms	39
Chapter Four	The Laying On of Hands	65
Chapter Five	The Resurrection of the Dead	85
Chapter Six	Eternal Judgment	109
Chapter Seven	The Elementary Doctrines and the Maturing Son	135
	Endnotes	141

WATCH SAM AND NICHOLAS SOLEYN SHARE FURTHER INSIGHT ON THE ELEMENTARY DOCTRINES.

INTRODUCTION
http://soleyn.com/elementary-doctrines/intro

REPENTANCE FROM ACTS THAT LEAD TO DEATH
http://soleyn.com/elementary-doctrines/dead-works

FAITH TOWARD GOD
http://soleyn.com/elementary-doctrines/faith-toward-god

BAPTISMS
http://soleyn.com/elementary-doctrines/baptisms

THE LAYING ON OF HANDS
http://soleyn.com/elementary-doctrines/laying-on-of-hands

THE RESURRECTION OF THE DEAD
http://soleyn.com/elementary-doctrines/resurrection

ETERNAL JUDGMENT
http://soleyn.com/elementary-doctrines/eternal-judgement

INTRODUCTION

A Culture of Maturity

There is perhaps no more intensive task one can choose to undertake than the raising of children. For parents, children are their posterity, with the potential to extend their destiny beyond their natural lifespan. Within the larger community, a child's maturation—choices made and the paths taken—reflect the culture of the people who influenced the child along the way, causing every member of the community to play some part in the child's development. Each generation builds from what was inherited from the previous one, and one cannot assess a generation's direction, accomplishments, or failures apart from those of the previous generations.

In the course of natural life, the inexorable passage of time makes this progression haphazard; for most families and communities, this connection between generations is unintentional.

In the Body of Christ, however, we all are sons of God. We come into the family of God through birth. Our initial stage is that of newborn children. As in natural families, there is an anticipated growth through various stages resulting in one becoming mature. We start as children whose growth and maturity is determined and stewarded by the head, the Lord Jesus Christ.

Christ has organized His Body as a multigenerational family. The foundation of this family is the Father-Son relationship, established by God as Father and as Son, and cultivated intentionally through spiritual fathers. The complete picture of this family is that of a Holy Nation that exists as one functioning Body under Christ's headship that displays the Kingdom of God in the earth.

The book *My Father! My Father!* by Sam and Nicholas Soleyn addresses this order, which Scripture refers to as the House of God in substantial detail.

The House of God refers to the family of God, which exists both in Heaven and on earth. As in the case of every family, the House of God has a unique culture. However, unlike natural human families, God's family derives its culture from God Himself. It is, therefore, a heavenly culture in the earth.

Though God's family comprises people from every nation, race, and background, His intent is that every person has a unique destiny through which he or she can display some facet of God's character. The goal is to put on display that aspect of God's character that he or she was put on the earth to represent as a son of God, irrespective of whether that person is male or female.[1]

Each individual is also part of the Body of Christ that as a whole is meant to display the fullness of God's personhood in the earth as the corporate Son. What ties the individual to the corporate, making the many one, is a culture that exists only in the Body of Christ.

Every believer's growth, from infancy to a functionally mature son of God, is a clear and defined process. As the education of a child exposes him or her to fundamental principles of thought and action, consistent with a family's culture and the goals of the greater society, so also the children of God must be exposed to the fundamental elements of the culture of Heaven and the greater structure of a Holy Nation.

The Elementary Doctrines are the building blocks of this culture, meant to be cultivated in the life of every believer. From infancy to maturity, these principles unfold with greater and greater complexity throughout the believer's life. The result is a unified corpus, with many parts, that is capable of presenting a standard of righteousness in the earth.

Introduction

Just as the individual believer must mature over time to more completely represent the Father, so too the corporate Son has been maturing through the many epochs of human history, moving closer to the full revelation of the Kingdom of God in the earth. *The Elementary Doctrines* are the foundation for a culture that brings about these kinds of maturity; one that is consistent with the culture of Heaven.

For the individual, *The Elementary Doctrines* lay a foundation for change. When one first chooses to follow Christ, that person begins a life of change—the constant changing of his or her nature, the changing of one's position within the Body as he or she matures, and the changing expression of one's destiny toward its complete expression.

Repentance From Acts That Lead to Death (Chapter One) is the first step in being born again of the Spirit and is also the basis for being established in spirit as a son of God, regardless of gender, race, or any other physical status.

Faith Toward God (Chapter Two) is the basis of a way of life that is consistent with belief and open to the economy of the Spirit to accomplish the things of God in the earth.

Baptisms (Chapter Three) are the procedures, both symbolic and experiential, that establish one's position in the Body of Christ with gifts and a calling.

The Laying On of Hands (Chapter Four) is the familial guidance one receives as he or she matures and changes position within the Body commensurate with that maturity, ultimately being confirmed and released to act with authority, both within the Body of Christ and the world.

The principle of *The Resurrection of the Dead* (Chapter Five) allows for the assemblage into the corporate Body, resulting in the release of one's destiny and a change in the individual from a perspective based in the natural to one that is informed by the Spirit.

Eternal Judgment (Chapter Six) is a further change in the expression of one's destiny as the position of the qualified judge is reserved only for the mature. Such judgments represent the stewardship of His House, affecting both mature and immature believers.

These teachings should be a continual presence in the believer's daily life. They should provide a place of reference, and at times reassurance, that what the believer experiences is part of the walk with Christ and His unfailing desire to bring each person to maturity.

These same teachings lay the foundation of a culture that identifies the functioning Body of Christ in the earth.

Repentance and the renewing of the mind is the foundation for receiving revelation and changing with the seasons over time. It is the basis by which the entire Body matures in its own destiny throughout the history of humankind.

Faith toward God is the foundation for a way of life that expresses the personhood of God in the earth, which is the continued work of Jesus Christ, the Son.

The different *Baptisms* are the mechanisms that give each part of the Body a complete destiny and refinement toward that destiny, yet allows each individual to take part in the complete revealing of God the Father in the earth.

The laying on of hands knits the Body together, giving function and support to each part.

The principle of the resurrection is the basis upon which the Spirit of Christ continues to operate in the earth through the assemblage of the sons of God.

Finally, *eternal judgment* is the result of a unified and mature corporate Son being present in the earth, having established the standard of righteousness by which all things may be judged and the taint of sin expunged from creation.

There is no reason any believer should remain perpetually an infant. Each person is meant to grow through specific stages of maturity. As sons of God, this process does not depend merely on the passage of time. Rather, this process depends upon the working of these principles throughout one's life as a believer. They represent both means for and the indications of reaching maturity.

The Foundation of Maturity

> *Therefore let us leave the elementary teachings about Christ and go on to maturity, not laying again the foundation*

of repentance from acts that lead to death, and of faith in God, instruction about baptisms, the laying on of hands, the resurrection of the dead, and eternal judgment. And God permitting, we will do so (Hebrew 6:1-3 NIV).

The basic Christian message that frames most believers' understanding of Scripture is that one must be saved from the consequences of sin, that he may go to Heaven when he dies, or conversely, that he may avoid hell. Apart from the initial message of salvation from sin, the believer's instruction typically focuses on the nature of good works, often emphasizing evangelism. The time between the person's salvation and death is meant for doing good works; the highest of which is to bring others to Christ, repeating the cycle.

This modern Christian message does not require a significant understanding of the Scriptures, nor does it require that the person who is saved become a mature son of God. The common church experience requires only basic familiarity with the particular doctrinal emphases of the church or denomination to which the believer is attached.

For example, traditional evangelicals favor topics related to salvation, evangelism, and good works as proof that they have had a born-again experience; those with a Pentecostal or Charismatic background tend to emphasize the topics of faith, money, power, and generally living the best version of one's life; and historic denominations ascribe particular importance to traditional church practices and being able to trace their roots back to important historical figures or events.

In each case, religious institutions and denominational groups have chosen easily consumable, narrow focuses at the expense of the depth of scriptural understanding necessary to build a foundation for wisdom in their leadership and maturity among their people.

Crises tend to expose the limitations of such selective emphases. National or international calamities inspire predictable responses. Those who emphasize going to Heaven immediately construe such events according to their anticipation of the end of the age and being raptured away. They will often make predictions around these topics, and they are routinely ridiculed in the media for their folly.

Others, those who emphasize good works, have generally relegated themselves to responding to disasters materially. They mobilize their resources by sending teams of relief workers into distressed areas to practice and show the caring nature of their evangelism, but their impact is no different than relief efforts conducted by secular groups. Whether they focus on escape or merely coping with the aftermath of disasters, the religious leaders' immaturity regarding their understanding of Scripture, beyond their own narrow imperatives, is made evident by their responses to these challenges.

The typical manner in which these groups respond to crises in individual believers' lives reveals the same shallow understanding. Usually, they will offer one of two explanations. The event is construed as either Satan's attack against the individual (either being provoked by efforts to spread the Gospel or simply as an attempt to hinder the person's walk of faith) or as God's displeasure with the person's behavior.

When they conclude that the person has offended God, the believer is encouraged to discover the offending condition and remedy it. When a crisis cannot easily be understood in terms of any moral failing—or such things as unfaithfulness in tithing or church attendance—there is an assumption as to the person's hidden motives or behaviors. The believer is blamed for any suffering she must endure. These responses do not offer the believer an explanation for the crisis based upon the solid foundation of Scripture, nor do they help the person understand the opportunities for growth and change inherent in these times of suffering.

Institutional religious models are based on the need of the institution to survive, regardless of the cost to the individual believer. Therefore, the messages are simple, basic, and uncomplicated, easily consumed and consensus building, so that the institution will survive by its appeal to the largest possible constituency. These messages present the ways of God as whimsical and unknowable, and God Himself may seem arbitrary and capricious. The people's continued unfamiliarity with God serves the institutions' investments in their limited topical emphases. The believer is not provided with training or an understanding of divine order by which he may consistently and accurately determine the will of God in any situation confronted in the world or in his life personally.

Often, believers will come to the place of questioning the doctrines, practices, and emphases of the religious institution, and often are they assured that the limitations they have discerned mark the furthest extent of truth available to human beings.

People should not be dissuaded from their search for truth by the dissatisfaction with the answers they receive from institutional and denominational leaders. The leaders are trying to hold on to authority rooted in the institution while the people are searching for greater spirituality. The religious world is in deep internal conflict, and this inward focus increasingly leads to outward irrelevance to society, generally, which increasingly operates apart from spiritual restraints.

The lack of maturity in both the leaders and the people has caused this dilemma. Even in questioning the models that they have left, many believers lack the foundation to ask the right questions. Their search for truth may be haphazard and unfocused. The solution is to build the foundation intended for every believer by which each person matures as a son of God.

The underlying cause of this immaturity is the systemic neglect of the Scriptures, particularly those regarding the foundations for maturity described in Hebrews 6:1 and 2. Believers, including leaders, are generally unfamiliar with these *Elementary Doctrines*.

The Elementary Doctrines

The author of the Book of Hebrews identifies six *Elementary Doctrines* that are the required foundation for the life of every believer: "repentance from acts that lead to death, and…faith in God, instruction about baptisms, the laying on of hands, the resurrection of the dead, and eternal judgment."[2]

The study and understanding of these doctrines lay the foundation of a believer's education that is required before one can, as the writer of Hebrews says, "go on to maturity."³ One must exercise much care to study and understand these doctrines. They form the basis of understanding of Scripture and revelation.

A believer should not expect to exhibit serious understanding, wisdom, and insight into the nature of God without having first developed the foundation for maturity by studying and employing the *Elementary Doctrines*. Similarly, a child does not start his educational career by reading the works of Shakespeare, Milton, and Tolstoy.

The Elementary Doctrines are analogous to a child learning the lessons taught in elementary school, designed to expose children to the basic skills by which they can communicate, interpret, and understand information, from the very basic application of these skills to the increasingly complex. The nature of the society in which a child grows up determines the basic skills he or she must develop to engage life within that culture as an adult.

These are called *Elementary Doctrines* because they form the substantial basis of a foundational education in the Scriptures, not because they are simple and easily grasped.

Beyond merely understanding these principles, the believer will experience challenges that allow him or her to implement the truth of these principles and bring light and wisdom to various circumstances. The Holy Spirit will reveal the mind of the Lord through these challenges. As the believer grows, circumstances will take on greater complexities to permit deeper understandings of these principles.

The Order of Maturity

Just as a person starts life as a small child and progresses through distinct stages to a mature adult capable of functioning in society, a son of God begins as one who is newly born again and progresses to being able to represent the interests of God the Father.

The designation "son of God" in Scripture not only has specific meaning regarding one's positioning in the will of God, it also has multiple distinct usages that denote one's level of maturity. To be a "son of God," one begins with the born-again experience, by which one is repositioned in Christ and enabled to be led by the Spirit.

Everyone who is born again has been given "the power to become sons of God."[4] Beyond this inceptive rebirth, there are various distinct usages of terms meaning "son" in Scripture that acknowledge the progression from a newborn to a mature son who represents his or her Father.[5]

A newborn believer is referred to by the term *nepios*, which refers to a son newly born into the family. However, when that son grows up and is competent to represent the interests of his father as a fully mature son, the designation *huios* is used appropriately to distinguish the fully mature son from the newborn infant.[6]

Between the newborn and the fully mature are other distinct specific stages of sonship, each referencing a growing level of maturity through which the believer progresses.

Maturity is defined by specific aspects of knowledge, understanding, and functionality, in increasing levels of complexity and responsibility.

Regarding their maturity, Paul wrote to the Corinthians, "I resolved to know nothing while I was with you except Jesus Christ and Him crucified."[7] He explained, "Brothers, I could not address you as spiritual but as worldly—mere infants in Christ. I gave you milk, not solid food, for you were not yet ready for it. Indeed, you are still not ready."[8]

Paul equated knowing nothing but Christ and Him crucified as "milk" for infants. He also equated their state of being infantile with them being "worldly" or "carnal."

Carnality means being motivated by the desires of the flesh and not the Spirit, causing one to be unable to make common and ordinary distinctions consistent with the life of a mature believer.

From Paul's assessment of the Corinthians, simply knowing Christ and Him crucified does not mean that a believer is mature; he made it clear that, without more, one is carnal and immature. This highlights the need for maturity as a prerequisite for receiving and understanding the wisdom that comes from God.

Paul taught that there is a message of wisdom, revealed by the Holy Spirit. Such wisdom, he wrote, can be given only to the mature:

> *We do, however, speak a message of wisdom among the mature, but not the wisdom of this age or of the rulers of this age, who are coming to nothing. No, we speak of God's secret wisdom, a wisdom that has been hidden and that God destined for our glory before time began* (1 Corinthians 2:6-7 NIV).

It is not the message of wisdom that makes believers mature, but rather, it is the foundational teachings and understanding that enable them to hear the message of wisdom. The goal is that every believer is able to represent the Father as a mature son of God. However, these concepts of maturity are largely absent from the thinking of believers today.

The Training of Believers in Christ

Even when believers select amongst the wide variety of teachers and publicized Christian materials, their learning is haphazard and without the appropriate structure to produce maturity. Having specific topical knowledge but lacking an overarching foundation for wisdom is a commonly recurring characteristic of believers that shows the result of this unstructured education.

The narrow emphasis on being saved and preparing to go to Heaven has produced a people who are generally unable to engage the world around them. The role of the Christian in society is seen as one who proselytes by offering a way of escape out of the troubles of the present world, and this limited Christian perspective deemphasizes the need for believers to meaningfully engage the society.

Howbeit, the *Elementary Doctrines* are a foundation upon which an entire way of viewing reality is structured. The employment of the *Elementary Doctrines* will result in growing up, from a newborn to becoming mature in Christ, leading one to a greater understanding of the events in the world and in one's personal life. These are not a set of distinctive doctrines relating to group membership. They are the pillars that support a distinctive way of life that enables the believer to represent God the Father and the reality of a transformed life.

CHAPTER ONE
REPENTANCE FROM ACTS THAT LEAD TO DEATH

Repentance is the means by which a person changes his or her nature from a sinful nature to one habitually dominated by the Spirit, implying also a changed mind-set.

In his letter to the Romans, Paul wrote, "Those who live according to the sinful nature have their minds set on what that nature desires; but those who live in accordance with the Spirit have their minds set on what the Spirit desires."[9]

Paul defined a sinful nature versus living in accordance with the Spirit each according to a particular mind-set. Therefore, the change from a sinful nature to a spiritual one is accomplished fundamentally by changing one's mind-set. This fundamental change of mind-sets refers to the conflict between a person's soul and spirit.[10]

The human being comprises three parts: the spirit, the soul, and the body.[11]

The spirit within human beings, originating out of the person of God as a gift from God Himself, is native to the world of God, that of spirit and of Heaven.[12] The soul bridges the gap between the natural world and that of the spirit, translating God's divine nature and eternal purposes to the natural world. God created mankind so that He would be seen and understood within the natural world. Making mankind spirit, soul, and flesh facilitates God's underlying purpose in putting His son into the earth.

The soul and the spirit each have three components: a mind, a will, and a heart. The mind collects and assimilates information upon which the spirit or soul bases its view of reality. The will assembles the resources available to the spirit or soul to interact with creation and actualize that reality. The heart supplies the motivation for the pursuit of the reality. In the intended harmonious functioning of the two, one's soul governs the actions of his body, and in turn, the mind, will, and heart of the soul are meant to be informed by and obsequious to the spirit.

The spirit is the part of a person's being that is in close fellowship and communion with God at all times.[13] The mind, will, and heart of the spirit are informed by the Holy Spirit. Therefore, when one is led by the Spirit, his view of reality is the same as God's view. This permits God to act vicariously through mankind and allows Him to be seen in the natural world.

The fall destroyed this elegant balance and freed the soul to act independently of the spirit. The decision to disobey God and the immediate consequences of that decision offer insight into the soul's process for making choices and its view of reality, in contrast to one being led by the Spirit.

> *When the woman saw that the fruit of the tree was good for food and pleasing to the eye, and also desirable for gaining wisdom, she took some and ate it. She also gave some to her husband, who was with her, and he ate it* (Genesis 3:6 NIV).

Eve chose to eat the fruit based on its appeal to the senses and the appeal of the enemy's argument that it would grant hidden wisdom.

This decision-making process contrasts the blind obedience to God, resulting from their complete trust in God, which had previously governed her and Adam's existence.

This obedience can be characterized as blind obedience because the eyes of their souls were closed, meaning the soul's mind, will, and heart that places mankind in competition with God had not yet corrupted their view of reality informed only by the Spirit of God. Once their souls' "eyes...were opened," their changed view of reality immediately asserted itself:

> [T]*hey realized they were naked; so they sewed fig leaves together and made coverings for themselves. Then the man and his wife heard the sound of the Lord God as He was walking in the garden in the cool of the day, and they hid from the Lord God among the trees of the garden. But the Lord God called to the man, "Where are you?" He answered, "I heard You in the garden, and I was afraid because I was naked; so I hid"* (Genesis 3:7b-10 NIV).

They no longer saw themselves as spirit beings, clothed in flesh, but instead saw themselves as only flesh, naked and vulnerable.

With this new vision of reality, their needs became focused on survival and their imperatives were provision and protection. Previously, they had known that they were spirit beings clothed in flesh and, therefore, not naked; and they had been familiar with God, who is also spirit.

Once mankind chose independence from God, the mind of the spirit, which is completely dependent on the Holy Spirit, was no longer the source of their information. Thus, they were limited to interpreting their physical surroundings to construct a view of reality. The only will by which they could function was their own. So, they provided for and protected themselves out of their own power, by fashioning clothing for themselves and hiding from God. And, they showed their changed hearts when they explained that they did these things out of fear. Human nature changed in that moment from one governed by the spirit to one governed by the soul.

Adam's actions interposed the mind, will, and heart of his soul between man's spirit and the Spirit of God, which had previously informed every aspect of mankind's being. The awakening and dominance of the soul was the consequence of choosing to live by a reality independent of God. The result was a changed view of reality and separation from God, the very description of sin. The loss of community with God also resulted in the loss of provision and protection supplied by the Spirit. Mankind assumed these twin burdens, which have become the primary imperatives continuously shaping human civilization.

As a consequence of the soul's awakening and independence, a person is capable of being of two differing mind-sets, as Paul taught in his letter to the Romans. There is a mind-set that is susceptible to sinful nature, and there is a mind-set that is in accordance with the Spirit. God gave human beings a spirit, out of His own person, so that they may be led by the Spirit of God:

> *For who among men knows the thoughts of a man except the man's spirit within him? In the same way, no one knows the thoughts of God except the Spirit of God. We have not received the spirit of the world, but the Spirit who is from God, that we may understand what God has freely given to us. This is what we speak, not in the words taught us by human wisdom but in words taught by the Spirit, expressing spiritual truths in spiritual words. The man without the Spirit does not accept the things that come from the Spirit of God, for they are foolishness to him, and he cannot understand them, because they are spiritually discerned* (1 Corinthians 2:11-14 NIV).

Only one who is led by the Spirit can know the mind of God. One who is not so led cannot. That person must have a different source of information, one that is confounded by spiritual things. "This wisdom descendeth not from above, but is earthly, sensual, devilish."[14]

The mind of the spirit is spiritually discerned, but the mind of the soul receives its information from three sources: the world, the flesh, and the devil.

As an example of the "wisdom" that is not spiritually discerned, Eve saw that the fruit on the tree was pleasing to the eye (sensual); she had the desire to possess the wisdom that it promised (earthly or worldly); and the information regarding the possibility of hidden wisdom was supplied from the devil, whose motivation was to seduce man from reliance upon the wisdom of God (devilish). These influences are not only susceptible to the enemy's manipulation but also exclude wisdom that comes from the Spirit of God. They are corrupt, and a mind-set that is based on these things is also corrupt.

When a person is dominated by his soul, he can harbor only a sinful nature, because the reality that determines his thoughts and actions is contrary to that which the Spirit of God would impart to the mind, will, and heart of the person's spirit. If one's thoughts and actions come from a reality that is not spiritually discerned, that person cannot also be led by the Spirit of God. This condition is properly defined as having a sinful nature.

When the Spirit of God informs the mind of a person's spirit, that person can understand both spiritual things and the natural world with God's wisdom. "The mind of sinful man is death, but the mind controlled by the Spirit is life and peace; the sinful mind is hostile to God. It does not submit to God's law, nor can it do so."[15]

Whereas the mind of the spirit is not susceptible to the enemy's deceptions, a mind dominated by sinful nature is hostile to God and unable to conform to God's will. The resulting behavior is "acts that lead to death."

Death, in this context, is best understood as a state of being separated from God.[16] Acts that lead to death are acts that separate a person from God. "God…made us alive with Christ even when we were dead in transgressions—it is by grace you have been saved."[17] Therefore, it is possible to be dead while yet alive.

Repentance from acts that lead to death is the elementary principle of changing one's mind-set from the view of reality inherited from Adam that opposes a way of life supported by the Spirit of God.

Christ accomplishes the first iteration of this principle when a person chooses to die to his or her inherited sinful nature and be born again of the Spirit. This first repentance represents the death of the right to direct one's own life. The changed mind-set comes from the changed sovereignty that governs one's life. This is the first step in the process of being born again and translated into the Body of Christ. (Note that this process also involves two of the Baptisms, which are discussed further in Chapter Three of this study series).[18]

This repentance begins the migration from the rule of self, susceptible to "the lust of the flesh, and the lust of the eyes, and the pride of life,"[19] to the rule of Christ and a nature that is habitually dominated by the Spirit of God.[20] "All this is from God, who reconciled us to Himself through Christ and gave us the ministry of reconciliation: that God was reconciling the world to Himself in Christ, not counting men's sins against them."[21] In Christ, we are assembled into one spiritual body, which means that we are reconnected to the spiritual reality of God Himself.

However, the complete change from soul to spirit is not accomplished immediately. Christ works out this change in each believer over time. Repentance from acts that lead to death is necessary both to overcome the schemes of the enemy and to mature as a son of God. This is a continually repeating process for individuals as they mature in Christ and for the corporate Son as new revelation from the Spirit of God matures the Body of Christ.

Acts that lead to death are inherently acts of sin. Paul taught, "For the wages of sin is death, but the gift of God is eternal life in Christ Jesus our Lord."[22] Such acts are not always overtly opposed to mandates plainly stated in Scripture. Many of the choices that lead to sinful acts are informed by a view of reality influenced by the "wisdom" of the world, the flesh, and the enemy's schemes. One's version of reality relates directly to that person's identity as a son of God.

Restoring the Identity of a Son

When mankind began to see itself as flesh and a different being from God, who is spirit, it lost the identity as sons of God. God is the Father of our spirits, and it is in our nature as spirits that we are sons of God.[23] When Adam hid from God, he rejected completely an identity associated with God. His mind-set shifted from being a son and heir of God to being merely a created being. He lost the identity of a son that was conferred upon him by his unique association with God.[24] When Adam was no longer informed by his spirit, he could not grasp a relationship to God, a spirit, as his Father. He became fatherless. Immediately, he set about supplying his own provision and his own protection, creating a culture of survival around these two imperatives. This new mind-set, which elevates self-provision and protection to its highest imperatives and is not connected to one's identity in his Father, created the culture of the orphan, which has dominated mankind's history.

Within the culture of the orphan, the imperatives of provision and protection nullify the mandates of a spiritual life. This culture may be so ingrained in an individual that these may not be conscious or overtly sinful choices. However, fear motivates and undergirds this culture, keeping the individual susceptible to the lusts of provision and protection, effectively separating that person from God.

The culture of the orphan is incompatible with the culture of a son. Satan introduced the culture of the orphan as an alternative to Adam's existence as a son of God. Satan himself is an angel, and like all angels, he was created to serve.[25] This culture is rooted in Satan's nature as a servant.

A servant can never understand the position of a son, since a servant does not have the relationship to God that a son has. Whereas a son is concerned with the representation of his father and he is the heir of all that his father has, a servant views his purpose as performing a task and gaining a consideration or reward. A servant looks for the mutuality of an exchange in which to find his value, and his goal is an equitable reward for his service. A son is unconcerned about his identity being related to the adequacy of his performance of a task. He already owns all his father has to offer. The son's primary intent is to accurately and exactly reflect the character of his father.

As a son of God, Adam was given to the representation of the interests of his Father, but his decision to separate himself from God rejected this divine purpose and ceded an identity of son related to God as Father. He opened himself to an identity based upon his performance.

God acknowledged that change when he said to Adam, "By the sweat of your brow you will eat your food until you return to the ground, since from it you were taken; for dust you are and to dust you will return."[26] God was not condemning Adam to a life of toil as punishment for his infraction; instead, God was acknowledging the natural consequences of Adam's choice. By rejecting his identity as a son, Adam's only other choice for an identity was that of a servant.

As a member of the Body of Christ, a believer who is a son is meant to model his life after Christ, the pattern Son. The Holy Spirit enables this way of life, while the conflict introduced in the garden highlights Satan's way of life.

Satan successfully deceived Adam into shifting his view of reality from spirit to soul, and son to servant and orphan. The shift in perspective was immediately evident as Adam's first subsequent acts were to provide for himself and protect himself by covering himself and hiding from God. He went from viewing God as a Father, to viewing Him as an enemy.

In that moment, mankind's relationship to God shifted from being sons to looking for the mutuality of exchange perceived in the arrangement by which man strives to please God in exchange for God's favor. The Holy Spirit does not enable a son of God's way of life within the culture of an orphan. Repentance and a changed mind-set enable the changing of one's culture as that person matures into a son who can represent God the Father by his or her way of life.

The Schemes of the Enemy

A believer is susceptible to the schemes of the enemy when the culture of the orphan continues to influence any areas of the person's life. Changing one's culture involves a process that must be worked out over time. This is why repentance and the changing of one's mind-set is a continually repeating process as a believer matures.

When a son is rightly aligned in his relationship to God, his spirit rules over his soul. When, however, he takes on the mind-set of an orphan, that balance is disturbed, resulting in the soul submerging the spirit with concerns related to provision and protection. The urgencies inherent in this pursuit leave a person open and susceptible to the enemy's suggestions. Whatever actions follow this pursuit inevitably separate the person from the life that is supported by the Spirit.

For believers, these pursuits are areas in which the person defaults to his or her own abilities and resources. The imperatives of provision and protection blind the individual to the identity and destiny as a son of God, highlighting the culture of the orphan as the basis by which one becomes separated from this identity and engages in acts that lead to death.

The act of repentance and returning to the mind-set of the spirit allows the Holy Spirit to expose the soul's dominance, which is the first step to regaining an identity as a son of God. One's identity as a spirit and son of God, and the dominance of the human spirit, which is derived from the Holy Spirit, negate the carnal, sensual, and devilish influences that would preoccupy the person with the overriding imperatives of provision and protection. This process frees the believer from the culture of the orphan and the prison of lusts and self-preservation. It repositions the son of God for the active pursuit of God with the goal of being reconciled to God Himself.

In any area where a person's soul is in preeminence over the spirit, the person is entrapped by the enemy's deceptions, even in his or her efforts to change. One may discern this condition in the revealing of the soul's nature governing the person's reality. The mind of the soul produces the orphan culture, defining itself apart from God as Father and seeking survival by the pursuits of provision and protection. The soul's will is to accomplish change through the person's own power or abilities. Moreover, the soul is motivated by fear, and all attempts to change one's condition that are rooted in the soul are motivated by fear of failure and loss. Without a change in mind-set, one may desire to change his sinful nature, but even in that desire, remain under the influence of the enemy.

When Is Repentance Necessary?

One of the many reasons to study the principles of repentance is to make one available to the revelation that repentance is necessary, either for one's self or to aid another. The need for repentance and a changed mind-set is revealed particularly through the condition of self-reliance for extended periods of time. A person in this condition develops learned responses motivated by fear.

Fear and an orphan culture make way for the world, the flesh, and the devil to influence the individual, often subtly. Self-preservation together with self-provision form the prison in which the person's soul is captured. The pursuit of these dual imperatives will highlight the enemy's schemes for the person inasmuch as the person's emotions and motivations exhibit a range of fears by which he or she makes decisions. This influence is interpreted correctly as demonic activity present in that person's life.

Although the average person exhibiting some or most of these traits may not be actually controlled by a demonic entity residing within the person, the broader sphere of demonic activity influences not only the person's view of life, but also the emotional responses that commonly accompany these views. A person may exhibit emotional paralysis, depression, hopelessness, despair, anger, and the like, as whole areas of the individual's life are controlled by fear. These are signs classically associated with demonic activity. Demonic activity should not be construed purely as related to the residence of a demonic presence within the body of a person, but should be considered in the wider ambit of the influence of demonically sourced conclusions and the emotions they stir. The remedy, however, is the same.

In order to overturn the effects of demonic activity within the life of a believer, it is necessary to restore the divine order of spirit over soul. This process begins with changing the mind-set from a servant or orphan back to that of a son.

As the son grows in maturity, he should be instructed in, and should learn to understand, the competing views of the soul and the spirit, learning to identify the mind-sets that make one susceptible to demonic influence and sin. Although much emphasis has been placed on deliverance (evicting a resident demonic presence), the failure to change the underlying culture of susceptibility to demonic influence leaves one delivered from the entity but still susceptible to the same influences that produced the infiltration in the first place.

Clearly, where a demonic presence has taken residence within one's soul, the remedy includes the eviction of the demon. However, if the house is cleaned and swept yet the underlying condition has not been remedied, the demon is apt to return, bringing his companions with him.[27] It is, therefore, necessary to deal with the underlying condition by which a person would remain open to attack and influence. That process results in the fundamental changing of the operative mind-set.

A believer must, therefore, be instructed personally in this process, because each person's susceptibility is as unique as the individual, and general instructions rarely produce an effective result. Every believer should have been introduced to this foundational precept as a means by which they could readjust their status, regularly, to reflect a correct alignment with the heavens and to keep from falling into the traps of the enemy, meant to impede the progress toward maturity. That is the normal growth path of a believer, and should be practiced routinely throughout one's life.

Repentance is inseparable from the practices associated with maturity. The enemy is unrelenting in his search for opportunity to hobble the believer; and as a son of God, each believer must be vigilant and unrelenting in rejecting these advances. The enemy will craft new and unique approaches, but he is limited by his nature as a servant. Moreover, his schemes are always based upon these familiar methodologies.

The Role of Spiritual Fathers

A necessary and indispensable aid to this process is having someone in the role of a spiritual father who keeps constant watch over one's soul and who helps identify the drift from the path of a son to that of an orphan. A spiritual father can discern and arrest the mind-set before it takes root and before the spiritual son recognizes the drift from his or her own path. And, a spiritual father is one who carries the grace and influence necessary to delve into the deep roots of fatherlessness and the orphan culture that make one open to the enemy's machinations.[28]

A spiritual father is one whose competence to do this is well advanced. John described a spiritual father as one who knows God the Father. Such a father is able to help younger sons of God to mature and overcome the schemes and deceptions of the enemy. John wrote, "I write to you, fathers, because you have known Him who is from the beginning. I write to you, young men, because you are strong, and the word of God lives in you, and you have overcome the evil one."[29]

This is a foundation of the order in the House of God for the maturing of His sons. Learning the stage of repentance from acts that lead to death is fundamental to one's maturing in Christ. And, repentance from acts that lead to death is necessary for avoiding, or engaging and overcoming, the enemy's efforts to separate a son of God from God the Father, after the son has been reconciled to God.

The change in one's identity, becoming a son of God, with a renewed mind-set is evident by the life the person lives. A son of God does not live as a slave or orphan. If someone claims to be a son yet lives as a slave, such a person has not embraced the next Elementary Doctrine, *Faith Toward God*. Where *Repentance From Acts That Lead to Death* begins and allows these changes, *Faith Toward God* provides the evidence of actual change while allowing the Spirit to work through the believer to affect change in his or her circumstances.

CHAPTER TWO
FAITH TOWARD GOD

What doth it profit, my brethren, though a man say he hath faith, and have not works? can faith save him? If a brother or sister be naked, and destitute of daily food, and one of you say unto them, Depart in peace, be ye warmed and filled; notwithstanding ye give them not those things which are needful to the body; what doth it profit? Even so faith, if it hath not works, is dead, being alone. Yea, a man may say, Thou hast faith, and I have works: show me thy faith without thy works, and I will show thee my faith by my works. Thou believest that there is one God; thou doest well: the devils also believe, and tremble. But wilt thou know, O vain man, that faith without works is dead? Was not Abraham our father justified by works, when he had offered Isaac his son upon the altar? Seest thou how faith wrought with his works, and by works was faith made perfect? ... Ye see then how that by works a man is justified, and not by faith only. ... For as the body without the spirit is dead, so faith without works is dead also (James 2:14-26 KJV).

Faith toward God is the second Elementary Doctrine in Hebrews 6:1-2. The author in this letter to the Hebrews reproved them, saying, "[T]hough by this time you ought to be teachers, you need someone to teach you the elementary truths of God's word all over again. You need milk, not solid food! ... [S]olid food is for the mature, who by constant use have trained themselves to distinguish good from evil."[30]

The understanding and constant use of these Elementary Doctrines allow every believer to "go on to maturity" in their relationship to Christ and His Body. The understanding and practice of faith toward God transitions one from the basic belief of "Jesus Christ and Him crucified," held by all believers, to a way of life that demonstrates the wisdom and power of Christ.

The importance of faith toward God lies in the understanding of Jesus's role in reconciling mankind to God the Father. "[Christ] is the image of the invisible God, the firstborn over all creation. ... But now He has reconciled you by Christ's physical body through death to present you holy in His sight, without blemish and free from accusation."[31]

The invisible God intended that He would be visible on earth through the Son. The earth would come to know the Father by the Son, and would have access to the Father through the Son.[32] This relationship required that the Son place His life entirely at the disposal of His Father, regardless of the demands upon that life. It required the Son's complete faith in the nature of His Father's love.

This pattern of life was meant to be replicated in each one who is also a son of God.

> *Now that faith has come, we are no longer under the supervision of the law. You are all sons of God through faith in Christ Jesus, for all of you who were baptized into Christ have clothed yourselves with Christ. There is neither Jew nor Greek, slave nor free, male nor female, for you are all one in Christ Jesus. If you belong to Christ, then you are Abraham's seed, and heirs according to the promise* (Galatians 3:25-29 NIV; see also Romans 8:15-17 NIV).

The elementary principle *Faith Toward God* defines faith within the context of this particular relationship to God. "[W]ithout faith it is impossible to please God, because anyone who comes to Him must believe that He exists and that He rewards those who earnestly seek Him."[33]

Faith is not a matter of placing hope in the unknown or the unknowable. It begins with a settled view that God exists, and within this context, God desires to live and be seen as a Father living through His son. Therefore, faith is more than belief in Jesus's death on the cross; it requires also a life patterned after Jesus's life on the earth.

The predicate of faith is God's word to His son. "Man does not live on bread alone, but on every word that comes from the mouth of God."[34] This word defines God's purpose for a person's life. A son of God will reveal God's invisible qualities in the life that God has articulated to him or her.

Everyone is born into the earth to fulfill a previously ordained divine purpose. This is confirmed repeatedly in Scripture. God told Jeremiah, "Before I formed you in the womb I knew you, before you were born I set you apart; I appointed you as a prophet to the nations."[35]

While Jesus was on trial for His life, He declared to the Roman governor Pontius Pilate, "…for this reason I was born, and for this I came into the world, to testify to the truth…."[36] God gave Joseph dreams in his youth that were fulfilled when he was thirty.[37] And, God "…set [Paul] apart from birth" to carry the word of the Lord to the Gentiles.[38]

God has designed a purpose for each person from before birth, choosing to make Himself visible uniquely through every person that chooses His way of life.

Faith toward God begins with the understanding that there is a unique life for which each person was put on the earth. Faith is the belief that God will support the existence He chose to have through each person. Faith toward God is a way of life consistent with that belief, choosing the path God designed.

Faith as a Way of Life

Current teachings on faith tend to serve the demands of the prevailing orphan culture.[39] From the perspective of the orphan culture, faith is a privilege to ask God for the things one desires. These requests tend to emphasize people's need for provision and protection: requests for material goods, physical healing, protection from evil, or the removal of obstacles. These are requests that a person believes would assure his or her survival. The efficacy of faith that serves an orphan culture depends upon the strength of one's conviction that God can and will fulfill the request. Ultimately, the empowerment of this version of faith and the desired results are determined by the individual.

Despite modern interpretations, faith toward God reflects the fundamental belief through a person's life that Jesus came from the Father to reveal His nature and restore God's original intent for creating mankind. It begins in believing in Jesus, as the Son who was sent.[40]

Christ Jesus put this model before us: "The Son is the radiance of God's glory and the exact representation of His being, sustaining all things by His powerful word. After He had provided purification for sins, He sat down at the right hand of the Majesty in heaven."[41] Faith toward God brings the same illumination to the world, exhibiting the authority and power of God in all of God's sons and in the corporate Son. Therefore, faith toward God is belief that is shown in a way of life patterned after Christ Jesus and His relationship to God the Father.

Faith as a way of life has two inseparable components: works and belief. James taught,

> *What good is it, my brothers, if a man claims to have faith but has no deeds? Can such faith save him? Suppose a brother or sister is without clothes and daily food. If one of you says to him, "Go, I wish you well; keep warm and well fed," but does nothing about his physical needs, what good is it? In the same way, faith by itself, if it is not accompanied by action, is dead* (James 2:14-17 NIV).

Belief as the foundation of a way of life, goes beyond an intellectual belief; it requires actions based on that belief. James further emphasized this point, saying,

> *But someone will say, "You have faith; I have deeds." Show me your faith without deeds, and I will show you my faith by what I do. You believe that there is one God. Good! Even the demons believe that—and shudder. ... As the body without the spirit is dead, so faith without deeds is dead* (James 2:18-19,26 NIV).

Belief alone is not a way of life, and works alone do not accurately represent the nature of God, because they do not evidence the belief that Christ will support the life He lives through each person.

People may perform great works apart from God, but these are not works of faith. Jesus taught, "He who speaks on his own does so to gain honor for himself, but he who works for the honor of the One who sent him is a man of truth; there is nothing false about him."[42]

Wealthy philanthropic persons or groups routinely outperform church organizations in measurable acts of goodwill. Some undertake relief projects that are global in scope, deploying an army of laborers in the service of mankind. They work to eradicate deadly diseases, improve education, and provide food and water to communities around the globe. These good works have come to vastly outstrip the collective efforts of church-based programs, but are unmotivated by faith.

The foundation known as faith toward God is choosing a way of life visibly based on the knowledge that God will support His intention to be made visible through His sons. One accomplishes this choice by modeling one's way of life after Jesus the Son and His relationship to God the Father. Therefore, Jesus taught, "My teaching is not My own. It comes from Him who sent Me. If anyone chooses to do God's will, he will find out whether My teaching comes from God or whether I speak on My own."[43] Christ is the pattern Son who demonstrated faith toward God by making the invisible God visible through Himself.

Faith as Substance and Evidence

What actions of the faithful person's way of life reveal God's invisible qualities? "Now faith is the substance of things hoped for, the evidence of things not seen."[44] Faith provides access into the substance of things hoped, defined, and supported by the evidence of things not seen. There is a body of evidence of the unseen world that gives shape to the actions one takes by faith.

There is a visible realm and an invisible realm. "By faith we understand that the universe was formed at God's command, so that what is seen was not made out of what was visible."[45] The realities of the invisible govern all events in the natural world. The substance that one's faith brings into the visible realm is determined completely by the invisible.

It is necessary to understand the invisible realm and the "evidence of things not seen," because it forms the basis for acts done by faith. Of course, the inability to observe this realm makes simply understanding it difficult—let alone accessing it. Functioning in the natural world according to invisible spiritual realities requires an understanding of the spiritual realm sufficient to enable a person to rely upon its existence. Accordingly, Scripture provides for the understanding of the relationship between the natural (visible) and the spiritual (invisible) realms.

The complete control that the invisible realm exerts over the visible shows an order of authority. The unseen world contains the higher order of authority than the world that man occupies, as evinced by the invisible realm's overarching influence.[46] However, mankind has access to authority even greater than the angels:

> *It is not to angels that He has subjected the world to come, about which we are speaking. ... "You made Him a little lower than the angels; you crowned Him with glory and honor and put everything under His feet." In putting everything under Him, God left nothing that is not subject to Him. Yet at present we do not see everything subject to Him* (Hebrews 2:5,7-8 NIV).

Faith Toward God

Where God has given mankind authority, He has done so from His throne, the Kingdom of Heaven. This authority is above the angelic, making "everything subject" to it; He is the Most High.

Within the invisible realm, there is also a place that demonic beings occupy. In dealing with the demonic, Jesus revealed the order of that dimension's authority. Though mankind is "a little lower" than even these angels, Jesus, His disciples, and others exert authority over them. Jesus explained, "…if I drive out demons by the Spirit of God, then the kingdom of God has come upon you."[47] Jesus commanded demons by the authority of the highest order, that of the Kingdom of Heaven.

More than just commanding the angelic hosts, faith toward God yields the substance of the invisible realm, made visible in the life of the believer. The substance of all he or she longs for resides in the realm that operates entirely by the nature and power of God. The believer, living a life based on faith, translates this substance into the natural realm.

However, access to God and to His realm requires that the person believe in the existence of God and that God is both interested and willing to appear within the circumstances with an intent to help with the problem. Therefore, to yield the substance of faith, the believer must be able to rely upon God's prior activities, indicating exactly this pattern of behavior on God's part. The evidence must show that there is an invisible world and a God over this invisible world whose nature is to love man and who has a pattern of visiting man to help him in his time of need.

Multiple examples in Scripture form the body of evidence that establishes exactly this pattern of behavior regarding God and His realm. The Scriptures record many of God's visitations with man, beginning with Adam and Eve in the garden of Eden and continuing throughout early human history.

These visitations provided the basis of faith for those whom God visited, and now, combined with their acts of faith, they provide all believers with a record of the pattern of God's interactions with mankind. Hebrews chapter 11 lists a sampling of the historic pattern by which mankind may rely upon God:

By faith Abel offered God a better sacrifice than Cain did. By faith he was commended as a righteous man, when God spoke well of his offerings. ...By faith Enoch was taken from this life, so that he did not experience death; he could not be found, because God had taken him away. ... By faith Noah, when warned about things not yet seen, in holy fear built an ark to save his family. By his faith he condemned the world and became heir of the righteousness that comes by faith. By faith Abraham, when called to go to a place he would later receive as his inheritance, obeyed and went, even though he did not know where he was going. ... By faith Abraham, even though he was past age—and Sarah herself was barren—was enabled to become a father because he considered Him faithful who had made the promise. ... By faith Abraham, when God tested him, offered Isaac as a sacrifice. He who had received the promises was about to sacrifice his one and only son, even though God had said to him, "It is through Isaac that your offspring will be reckoned." ... By faith Isaac blessed Jacob and Esau in regard to their future. By faith Jacob, when he was dying, blessed each of Joseph's sons, and worshiped as he leaned on the top of his staff. By faith Joseph, when his end was near, spoke about the exodus of the Israelites from Egypt and gave instructions about his bones. By faith Moses' parents hid him for three months after he was born, because they saw he was no ordinary child, and they were not afraid of the king's edict. By faith Moses, when he had grown up, refused to be known as the son of Pharaoh's daughter (Hebrews 11:4-5,7-8,11,17-18,20-24 NIV).

In the New Testament, a similar abundance of evidence exists. However, concerning God's reliability to appear for the benefit of mankind, Jesus is the preeminent evidence.[48] This evidence is more than sufficient for believers to rely on the truth of the existence of the invisible realm, subject to the control of God.

Even though God Himself is invisible, His interactions with mankind leave no doubt as to His existence and of His intent to ascribe a destiny and fulfill it in every person who chooses Him. Faith toward God is formed on the belief that in God exists all the substance that supports each person's unique identity in Christ upon the earth. Faith enables the economy of the Spirit, providing access into that substance and supported by the evidence of things not seen.

The Economy of the Spirit

God designed an economy to enable His purposes in the earth. God decrees an eternal purpose, and the Holy Spirit supplies the power of Christ sufficient to support that decree. The economy of the Spirit describes the dispensation of authority and power into human circumstances to enable God's decrees from Heaven.

Certain religious circles have stripped the term *dispensation* of its basic meaning—namely to dispense or to distribute—and made it into a term of art with a specific and quite different meaning. As a term of art, they use it to mean a time period or an epoch during which God fulfilled a certain promise. This specialized usage of the term *dispensation* is conspicuously lacking in support from any reading of the Scriptures, as well as normal usage. It is an inaccurate invention, mostly designed to support an unbiblical bias.

Instead, a dispensation is a giving out or a distribution of an economy, designed to support a heavenly initiative, thereby guaranteeing the success of that initiative. The word *economy* is derived from the Greek *oikonomos*, comprising the terms *oikos* (meaning "house") and *nomos* (meaning "law" or "custom").[49] God established His house as the economy by which the Spirit operates in the Body of Christ. This dispensation takes the form of an increased increment of the order of God's house.

The story of Jesus walking on the water illustrates the economy of the Spirit:

The Elementary Doctrines

> *When evening came, His disciples went down to the lake, where they got into a boat and set off across the lake for Capernaum. By now it was dark, and Jesus had not yet joined them. A strong wind was blowing and the waters grew rough. When they had rowed three or three and a half miles, they saw Jesus approaching the boat, walking on the water; and they were terrified. But He said to them, "It is I; don't be afraid." Then they were willing to take Him into the boat, and immediately the boat reached the shore where they were heading* (John 6:16-21 NIV).

This story shows the contrast between the economy of the Spirit and the human economy. The disciples' efforts, rowing against the wind and making little progress, represent the standard economy of man—toil and effort being resisted by adversity, and success coming through persistence. People have operated according to this economy since the fall.[50] Humans have evolved an economy based on one's efforts, relegating God to a helper who might change the variables that frustrate a person's toil. This economy has given rise to those teachings on faith that seek to fulfill personal desires for provision and protection.

The fact of a man walking on the water introduced a different economy.

Jesus approached the disciples in the boat as they were toiling against the opposing gale, presenting a side-by-side depiction in which the familiar economy existed with the spiritual. Jesus and His disciples left from the same port, going the same direction.

Although Jesus started later than they did, the wind had arrested the boat's progress, and Jesus, being unaffected, overtook them and was about to go past them. Jesus was operating in a different economy, though both He and the disciples were in the same place at the same time.

The effect that Jesus's spiritual economy had on the natural realm was shown when He entered the disciples' boat. Had Jesus walked past, one might conclude that the two economies operated fully apart from each other. However, the disciples invited Him into their boat and "immediately the boat reached the shore where they were heading." Jesus carried His economy with Him always and converted their economy to His, thereby conferring the benefits of His economy to their human circumstances.

The coexisting realities of the eternal and the natural are attended by separate and distinct economies, but the eternal economy of the Spirit will always encompass and change the circumstances of the natural realm, transporting it into the economy of the Spirit. The result is defined as miraculous. It elevates the natural to the plane of the spiritual, and in this transcendence, the impossible becomes the possible.

Faith toward God produces an unshakable confidence in the reality of God. The mature House of God functions in the world, according to the Spirit, by the certainty of God and total confidence in Him. This unshakable confidence sustains the believer's way of life.[51]

Higher and Lower Authorities

The dominant reality governing the circumstances of human existence in the visible world originates in the unseen spiritual world.[52] All things that effect humanity originate in the invisible world. "So we fix our eyes not on what is seen, but on what is unseen. For what is seen is temporary, but what is unseen is eternal."[53] When operating among the unseen realms, faith is required, because humans are reluctant to embrace anything that may not be empirically ascertained as reality.

Mankind exists in the natural, visible realm, but humans are spirit beings clothed in a body made of dust. A person's essential nature transcends the natural realm. However, one's comprehension of the spiritual realm is limited to that which the Holy Spirit imparts to his or her spirit. This knowledge is not complete, because the Holy Spirit imparts that knowledge necessary for a person's purpose. For example, a person ought to know the God-ordained purpose for his or her life; and one should also possess sufficient knowledge of the order and function of the spirit realm.

These truths are veiled to those whose perspective is dominated by the mind of the soul, because after the fall, when the eyes of the human soul were opened, it no longer viewed itself as spirit clothed in flesh, but as flesh only.[54] However, for one led by the Spirit, the Spirit will supply the knowledge that allows one to operate in the natural world as a spirit being and permits one to decide what things are from God and what comes from the enemy. Therefore, by faith and the economy of the Spirit, people are capable of putting on display realities of the eternal realm in the natural realm, because they are spirits held in place in the natural realm by physical bodies.

Faith involves the interaction between both realms. The higher realm is the spiritual, and the order of that realm governs the lower realm of earth.[55] A way of life based on faith allows access into the spiritual realm to receive the economy that supports God's purposes for a person.

The need for mankind to engage the spiritual realm exists because there is a conflict that spans the visible and invisible worlds. The highest order, occupied by the throne of God, is the third heaven.[56] This is the dwelling place of God and His angels, and His authority supports the Kingdom of Heaven in both Heaven and earth. Satan and his angels fell to a place lower in authority than the third heaven and are in conflict with the throne of God. [57] Being in conflict with the throne of God, Satan and his forces also resist the advent of God's Kingdom into the earth, the lowest of the realms.[58]

Ultimately, Satan's realm and mankind's realm are subject to the authority of the throne of God, the Most High. Accordingly, God Himself may summon Satan to appear to give an account.[59] Similarly, Satan asks permission to conduct his activities on the earth.[60] The authority that comes from Heaven trumps any human or demonic claims of authority in any of the realms.

Mankind, whose purpose is to represent God, will encounter the demonic forces and must understand that certain rules of engagement apply. Dealing with the demonic represents a conflict between humans and creatures of a higher dimension.

The human is in the least powerful position. If one attempts to revoke a demon's claim of authority—to inhabit a person, for example—one should realize that the demon has used superior knowledge to assert its claim. The believer engaging the demonic must access the authority from the throne of God. The economy that follows will place the demonic being's claim of authority against the truth of the power and authority of the Kingdom of Heaven, revealed by the Spirit and supported by the throne of God. As a representative of God's Kingdom, the human can revoke the demonic's claim to authority.[61] Therefore, it is by the authority of the throne of God that humans overcome demonic intrusions and influences.

Faith in Practice

God has deployed His sons into time and space to represent the interests of His Kingdom. The sons of God bring the order of the Father's Kingdom into the lowest of the dimensions. The enemy opposes this order and operates from a place greater in power and authority than mankind. To represent God the Father, believers must be keenly aware of the authority by which they function. Faith toward God in practice is a person's operation from the base of the highest authority.

Faith is in operation because the representation of God the Father greatly contrasts, and is often opposed to, human constitutions of authority. For example, if a person or group leads by the consent of the populous, that leadership may succeed against earthly oppositions, because they are on a level playing field. However, the populous has no power or authority to affect the demonic, and consequently, the leadership cannot be empowered to engage influence coming from the demonic forces. This is true whether people are aware of their opposition's activities or not.

Where this structure is further afflicted by the orphan culture that predominates human governments, faith becomes merely an additional means of supply and protection.

A son of God does not need to supply his or her own provision and protection. The son represents the Father, and God the Father already knows all a person will need to succeed in that representation.

Faith toward God relieves a person of the burdens of provision and protection. Regarding the measure of one's faith as viewed by his or her imperatives, Jesus taught:

> *"So do not worry, saying, 'What shall we eat?' or 'What shall we drink?' or 'What shall we wear?' For the pagans run after all these things, and your heavenly Father knows that you need them. But seek first His kingdom and His righteousness, and all these things will be given to you as well"* (Matthew 6:31-33 NIV).

Faith toward God means that the son of God is preoccupied with the advance of His Father's interests in the earth.

Faith requires belief in the existence of the invisible apart from the fact that it cannot be seen. A mature son of God will live according to a belief in the existence of God though that existence cannot be seen or measured by material circumstances. Consequently, by God's will, a spiritual economy will empower the actions of a son of God who is sufficiently mature to call upon the Kingdom of Heaven's resources in furtherance of God's purposes in the earth.

The mature son has clarity about his role of representing the Father. Jesus, the fully mature Son, had an active communication with God, and everything He prayed for was answered. Even in His prayer to be spared the suffering He would endure, Jesus was consistent with the will of God.[62]

One should not be distracted by God's willingness to directly answer the request of an immature son, however. He does so often. In spite of this fact, some insist that the immature son does not receive a consistent answer to his prayers, because he has not learned, nor does he practice consistently, the appropriate formulas for coaxing God into a consistent benevolent response.

The truth, however, is that the immature son often vacillates between the culture of an orphan and that of a son, yet God supplies the need for that person to transition fully into the culture of a son.

This need often includes God directly answering the immature son's requests. Faith builds maturity.

Faith, as a way of life, is patterned after Jesus. Jesus described the standard of faith as "[T]he Son can do nothing by Himself; He can do only what He sees His Father doing, because whatever the Father does the Son also does."[63]

The substance of His relationship with the Father was both His identity and the foundation upon which He engaged the throne of God. Jesus paid complete attention to the will of His Father, being secure in the knowledge that whatever He needed of a material sort would be added routinely.[64] The evidence of that reality was His way of life that routinely put on display the power and authority that flowed from the throne of God, and His connection as a Son to His Father. He never occupied Himself with any request for a material consideration. He focused exclusively on representing His Father on the earth. He was routinely opposed by the enemy, but experienced the Father's superintending care. The ultimate expression of Jesus's faith and His Father's unbending willingness to support His Son was Christ's resurrection from the dead.

Faith and Maturity

Faith is based upon the certainty of a relationship with God that provides an economy upon the earth in which a son may live in complete reliance. Absent that clarity of understanding, a believer may experience answers to his prayers for provision and protection, but whenever those requests contradict the eternal purposes of God for his life, the believer experiences the disappointment of an unfulfilled request. This fact, combined with a paucity of spiritual guidance, has often led people to uncertainty and a somewhat tepid reliance on God.

To rehabilitate the doctrine of faith toward God, every believer should be taught from the beginning that faith is built upon the reality of God as his or her Father and that every person was put on the earth to represent God the Father. The substance of the relationship between mankind and God is the foundation upon which the son relies for his well-being and empowerment. That relationship proves itself consistently with the growing evidence of divine intervention, experienced sporadically at the beginning of one's life as a believer and becoming routine through the various stages of maturity. The evidence of both the eternal reality and divine power will accumulate in the life of the believer through the various stages of growth, from infancy to maturity, and throughout the person's lifetime.

Every believer has been fitted with a particular destiny that requires divine empowerment in order for that destiny to succeed. The maturing process brings greater clarity to the exact nature of that eternal purpose together with the person's functioning according to that purpose. With this functioning necessarily comes a greater reliance upon the economy of God. Eventually, faith toward God will become the mature son's way of life.

CHAPTER THREE

BAPTISMS

The next Elementary Doctrine mentioned in Hebrews is the instruction about *Baptisms*. Baptisms, in Scripture, are administrative processes of change. They require an administrator, one who is different from the believer undergoing the changes. Each baptism affects the position of the believer—with respect to the heavenly realms, the person's own destiny, the Body of Christ, and the person's positioning, or relative maturity, as a son of God—making instruction about baptisms a vitally important point of reference as these changes are administered.

Scripture contains four distinct baptisms: baptism in water (see Rom. 6:1-2 NIV); the baptism *of* or *with* the Spirit (see Luke 3:16; Acts 1:5 NIV); the baptism *by* the Spirit (see 1 Cor. 12:12-13 NIV); and the baptism of fire, also known as the baptism of suffering (see Luke 3:16; 1 Cor. 3:13; Acts 2:3 NIV). With respect to each other, there is not a specific chronological order to the baptisms. They administer change in the life of a person, beginning from a newborn believer and through the stages of maturity. Accordingly, the need for each baptism depends upon the state of the individual. As an Elementary Doctrine, "instruction about baptisms" is a necessary foundation for stewarding an individual's maturity in Christ and participating in the maturing and functioning corporately of the Body of Christ.[65]

Order of Baptisms

Baptisms bring change from one condition to another through different stages of a person's life. These stages occur from person to person variously—there is no set way by which each person comes to Christ; and each person has a unique calling, is a specialized part of the Body of Christ, and is brought to maturity through trials that complement the person's identity in Christ. Stages of believers' lives are not identical, and neither are the baptisms' administrations of change.

The order in which a person experiences each of the four baptisms follows the spiritual condition of the individual. In Scripture, some were first baptized with the Holy Spirit before they were baptized in water.[66] Others were first baptized with water followed by the baptism of the Spirit.[67] The baptism of fire is administered at different times in the life of a believer and is associated with growth and progress toward spiritual maturity.[68] The remaining baptism, the baptism by the Spirit, is the assembling of all believers into one body and occurs when the person is born again of the Spirit.[69] The circumstances of a person's life determine the changes required through the stages of maturity.

God enjoins the spiritual process according to an individual's heart and circumstances. Examples of this order abound throughout Jesus's ministry. The story of Zacchaeus is one illustration:

> [Zacchaeus] *wanted to see who Jesus was, but being a short man he could not, because of the crowd. So he ran ahead and climbed a sycamore-fig tree to see Him, since Jesus was coming that way. When Jesus reached the spot, He looked up and said to him, "Zacchaeus, come down immediately. I must stay at your house today." So he came down at once and welcomed Him gladly. All the people saw this and began to mutter, "He has gone to be the guest of a 'sinner.'" But Zacchaeus stood up and said to the Lord, "Look, Lord! Here and now I give half of my possessions to the poor, and if I have cheated anybody out of anything, I will pay back four times the amount." Jesus said to him,*

"Today salvation has come to this house, because this man, too, is a son of Abraham" (Luke 19:3-9 NIV).

Jesus engaged Zacchaeus from the point where He met Zacchaeus in the tree. He discerned from Zacchaeus's climbing into the tree that he had already repented of his way of life. A man of small stature who was also a member of the hated tax-collecting profession would not normally have exposed himself to the ridicule of the crowd by climbing into a tree. His desire to see the Lord was greater than his fear of ridicule. From this act, one could conclude properly that Zacchaeus had already repented. Accordingly, Jesus simply invited Zacchaeus to lunch at the tax collector's house.

Jesus operated by discerning people's hearts and showing them the love of the Father based upon their unique needs. Typically, repentance is the first step toward sonship, but in this story, there is no reference to any process of Zacchaeus's repentance or confession. There was no need for Zacchaeus to verbalize the active condition of his heart; the evidence became apparent when he offered to refund four times the monies he had taken unjustly. The Lord's actions signify that Zacchaeus's sins were already forgiven. This pattern models the need for discernment to show a person the Father's love according to his or her unique circumstances.[70]

Discerning people's hearts and circumstances as Jesus did precludes religious formulae for baptisms and their administrations. All the baptisms are necessary for every believer. However, the manner of their administration depends on the individual's needs. Discernment of the Spirit, then, is the necessary prerequisite for determining timing of the various baptisms in each person's life.

Baptism in Water

As the progenitor of mankind, Adam's legacy is an identity separate from God the Father, into which each person is born. A consequence of this identity in Adam is that one is subject to the rule of Satan, the *Kosmokrator*, and his kingdom, the *Kosmos*.[71]

In the Gospel of the Kingdom of God, the need to change one's location from the kingdom of darkness to the rule of Christ is the central message. Before one can come under Christ's rule as a citizen of the Kingdom of God, the person must be separated from the identity in Adam and the enemy's authority. This separation occurs with the death of that identity and the birth of a new creation.

Water baptism is an important part of this process. Removing the old identity and being adopted into the Kingdom of Heaven involves a person's symbolic death, burial, and resurrection.

> *What shall we say, then? Shall we go on sinning so that grace may increase? By no means! We died to sin; how can we live in it any longer? Or don't you know that all of us who were baptized into Christ Jesus were baptized into His death? We were therefore buried with Him through baptism into death in order that, just as Christ was raised from the dead through the glory of the Father, we too may live a new life. If we have been united with Him like this in His death, we will certainly also be united with Him in His resurrection. For we know that our old self was crucified with Him so that the body of sin might be done away with, that we should no longer be slaves to sin—because anyone who has died has been freed from sin* (Romans 6:1-7 NIV).

Specifically, baptism in water represents a burial.

Repentance precedes water baptism because repentance represents death in the process. Repentance results in a changed mind-set from the individual's innate desire to control all aspects of his or her own life. Through repentance, the individual sacrifices the imperatives of self-provision and protection that are the legacy of an identity in Adam.

Fundamentally, repentance changes the sovereignty that governs one's life. Prior to accepting Christ's sovereignty, one is governed by self-originating imperatives, subjugating a person to the rule of lusts—the lust of the flesh, the lust of the eyes, and the pride of life.[72] These lusts, in turn, provide a means for Satan to establish control over the person's life.[73] Through repentance, a person migrates from the rule of self and Satan to the rule of Christ and begins the transfer from the "dominion of darkness" into the Kingdom of Heaven.[74]

Water baptism is a burial of the old self, which is followed by one's resurrection as a new creation. "[I]f anyone is in Christ, he is a new creation; the old has gone, the new has come!"[75] When one repents, is buried, and then is raised as a new creation, that person is removed from the jurisdiction and control of the kingdom of darkness. The person is instead adopted as a child of God, a son and heir of the Kingdom of God. This adoption places the individual under the rule of Jesus Christ, the King.

The importance of water baptism is the declaration to the heavens that the new creation is not subject to the enemy's accusations of sin. There is an entire, powerful kingdom arrayed in opposition to Christ and His Kingdom.[76] The enemy employs false accusations presented as truth against those born again and adopted into the Kingdom of Heaven. Even when he no longer has control over a person, the enemy will still seek to reassert influence over that person's life. He does this by attempting to define the person by his or her previous sinful nature, before being raised as a new creation.

These attacks are against the mind of the human soul. A person may be "in [one's] mind…a slave to God's law, but in the sinful nature a slave to the law of sin."[77]

The enemy selects moments of weakness when a person thinks or acts in a manner similar to the person's previous life. These false accusations take on the appearance of truth, because they are typically timed to exploit some occasion of weakness or sin. Acquiescence to the lie that one's life before Christ bears any influence on Christ's sovereignty over the person or God's love for His children leaves that person open to further demonic influence.

In these attacks, only the truth regarding the sovereignty over a person's life restrains the enemy. The truth is that…

> *...if anyone is in Christ, he is a new creation; the old has gone, the new has come! All this is from God, who reconciled us to Himself through Christ and gave us the ministry of reconciliation: that God was reconciling the world to Himself in Christ, not counting men's sins against them.... God made Him who had no sin to be sin for us, so that in Him we might become the righteousness of God* (2 Corinthians 5:17-19,21 NIV).

Everyone belongs to either the Kingdom of God or the kingdom of darkness and is therefore subject to Christ's sovereignty, or Satan's.[78] Those who have not been raised as a new creation are subject to "the rulers of the darkness of this world."[79]

> *As for you, you were dead in your transgressions and sins, in which you used to live when you followed the ways of this world and of the ruler of the kingdom of the air, the spirit who is now at work in those who are disobedient. All of us also lived among them at one time, gratifying the cravings of our sinful nature and following its desires and thoughts. Like the rest, we were by nature objects of wrath. But because of His great love for us, God, who is rich in mercy, made us alive with Christ even when we were dead in transgressions—it is by grace you have been saved. And God raised us up with Christ and seated us with Him in the heavenly realms in Christ Jesus* (Ephesians 2:1-6 NIV).

This makes one vulnerable to the accusations that the enemy brings. But, "there is now no condemnation for those who are in Christ Jesus, because through Christ Jesus the law of the Spirit of life set me free from the law of sin and death."[80]

Water baptism is a declaration that the person being baptized is under the rule of Christ. Through the act of baptism, the person is dead and buried. The only way forward is through resurrection. The person coming through this process begins a new life as a resurrected being and a new creation. There is no truth in any condemnation of sin rooted in the old life, and through the continual process of repentance and the renewing of the mind, the person is freed from the consequences of sin.[81]

There are times when water baptism is appropriate for a believer who has already repented and received the Holy Spirit. [82] If the believer struggles with accusations of thoughts or behaviors that come from the person's old life, or if the person struggles to believe consistently that "the old is gone, the new has come!" that person should consider being baptized in water.[83]

This baptism, in order to simulate burial, should be by immersion, and it should be administered only to an adult who is capable of choosing to be baptized and distinguishing between truth and error.

Water baptism declares to the heavenly realms that the person baptized has died to the old self and has been buried, negating the enemy's authority in any aspect of the person's life from that point forward. Memories and other familiarities with the old life do not amount to a reconnection to that life and are invalid bases for condemnation from the enemy. The person who now lives is a new creation subject only to the authority of Christ.

Water baptism establishes by symbolic burial that the believer has chosen consciously to come under the rule of Christ: "The like figure whereunto even baptism doth also now save us (not the putting away of the filth of the flesh, but the answer of a good conscience toward God,) by the resurrection of Jesus Christ."[84] Having repented, been buried, and been resurrected from the dead, a person leaves behind the kingdom of darkness, Satan's rule, and the state of death that is separation from God.

Baptism in water, generally, should occur as part of the process by which a person is translated into the Kingdom of Heaven. This process begins with repentance, in which a person dies to his or her identity in Adam, and it includes the symbolic water baptism performed person to person.[85] Having made a conscious decision, called repentance, each person has an advocate in Christ to establish the fact that they are free from condemnation before God.[86] The process culminates with one's resurrection as a new creation, confirmation of one's identity, and being baptized with the Holy Spirit.[87] Therefore, though symbolic, water baptism is a necessary foundation for one's introduction into the Kingdom of Heaven and for stewarding the growth and maturity of the children of God.

Baptism of the Spirit

The previous section on water baptism discussed the process of being reborn as a new creation. As with any new birth, there is a process of maturing. This deliberate process brings a person through various stages of maturity, from a newborn to a son of God who is fit to represent his Father. The Holy Spirit equips a person with the gifts necessary to succeed at whatever level of representation the person occupies at any given stage. God intends to bring everyone whom He receives as a son to maturity, so that they may fulfill the destiny for which He created them.

God designed each person uniquely to display some facet of His nature in the earth, and the baptism of the Spirit confers the requisite power for this calling as a son of God. The baptism of the Spirit is a baptism of power, and it accompanies the transition one makes from being an orphan to becoming a son of God.

This distribution of the power comes in the form of spiritual gifts.[88] Paul confirmed that the gifts of the Spirit, though varying in function, serve a unified goal:

> *There are different kinds of gifts, but the same Spirit. There are different kinds of service, but the same Lord. There are different kinds of working, but the same God works all of them in all men. Now to each one the manifestation of the Spirit is given for the common good* (1 Corinthians 12:4-7 NIV).

The "common good," as Paul names it, is the singular intent of God, embodied in the Spirit, accomplished uniquely through each son of God and corporately through the Body of Christ.[89]

Christ endows each believer with His power and authority in a manner that will allow the person to represent Christ uniquely, and fully, as a member of the Corpus. God's original intent for mankind will be made complete through the Body of Christ. To that end, Christ claimed plenary authority declaring, "All authority in heaven and on earth has been given to Me."[90] Christ gives His power over to His corporate Body through the Holy Spirit:

> *But when He, the Spirit of truth, comes, He will guide you into all truth. He will not speak on His own; He will speak only what He hears, and He will tell you what is yet to come. He will bring glory to Me by taking from what is Mine and making it known to you. All that belongs to the Father is Mine. That is why I said the Spirit will take from what is Mine and make it known to you* (John 16:13-15 NIV).

There is no other way to receive the power of Christ than through His delegate, the Holy Spirit. Christ appended to His declaration of complete power and authority the Great Commission to His disciples.[91] He fully intended to support these activities with power. Otherwise, the Gospel they preached would yield no change among mankind.[92] There is no other way to accomplish the things of God than with the power of Christ.

Christ baptizes with the Holy Spirit, and the Holy Spirit administrates His power. Christ established His Kingdom and made us its ambassadors. The authoritative foundation of His Kingdom recognizes a grant of authority from the Father— "All authority in heaven and on earth has been given to Me."[93] Our power to act as ambassadors of this Kingdom and as representatives of the Person of God Himself comes from this source of authority. We are introduced to this authority by the baptism of the Spirit. Unlike water baptism, which is administered by one person to another, the baptism of the Spirit is exclusively administered by Christ Himself, since He is the only one capable of imparting divine authority to His representatives.

No one was ever baptized in the Spirit until Jesus returned to Heaven. John the Baptist prophesied of Christ, "I baptize you with water for repentance. But after me will come one who is more powerful than I, whose sandals I am not fit to carry. He will baptize you with the Holy Spirit and with fire."[94]

After Jesus was resurrected, before ascending to Heaven, He referenced John's prophetic declaration, commanding the apostles to abide in Jerusalem saying, "…wait for the gift My Father promised, which you have heard Me speak about. For John baptized with water, but in a few days you will be baptized with the Holy Spirit."[95] The first instance of this baptism took place on the Day of Pentecost after Jesus returned to Heaven.

The baptism of the Spirit is for empowerment. The baptism of the Spirit is not just for the impartation of gifts of power, but an enabling power toward specific ends. "[Y]ou will receive power when the Holy Spirit comes on you; and you will be My witnesses in Jerusalem, and in all Judea and Samaria, and to the ends of the earth."[96]

Jesus not only told His disciples that they would receive power, but said that they would be His witnesses in the earth. Power is meant to enable functioning. We are commissioned to continue Christ's work on the earth. Just as He was empowered to represent the Father, we are also empowered by the same means to continue the same work.

However, whether by religious prejudice or simply the lack of proper information, the individual may reject the power of the Spirit. For example, religious groups who believe in the indwelling of the Holy Spirit may, on the basis of theological bias, limit the activities of the Spirit. Some groups reject healing or tongues or various other manifestations of the Spirit's power. However, whenever the Holy Spirit is present in a person, He comes with all that He is, including the ability to distribute endowments of the power of Christ, sufficient to enable the person to fulfill a divine calling.

It is a common phenomenon to discover groups of people who believe in the indwelling of the Holy Spirit but who lack any significant empowerment. In such cases, power to accomplish religious objectives comes from the group, while at the same time they lack any divine reference or supernatural character. Such groups rely upon the goodwill of the people, and the leaders spend most of their time building consensus and stirring up the people to participate on the basis of duty and human goodwill. Such efforts appeal to the soul and lack the characteristics of divine intervention. When, however, people are open to being filled with the power of the Spirit of God, they may be empowered by the authority of Christ.

Gifts of the Spirit match not only one's level of representation but also his or her unique commission.[97] Christ grants sufficient power and authority to accomplish all that He intends. Gifts of the Spirit result also in a cultural change from an orphan to a son. This opens the way for a maturity that corresponds to the changing stages of sonship.

As one grows from the stage of an infant to a fully mature son, greater power and authority are conferred upon the person together with greater responsibility. Paul instructed people to "eagerly desire the greater gifts," because this is the natural and intended progression for every son of God.[98]

The Administrations of the Holy Spirit

Power derived from the baptism of the Spirit falls into three basic categories of gifts, which the Spirit administers for different purposes. These forms of gifts are (1) administrations of power through sudden appearances (_phaneros_), e.g., Acts chapter 2 (the Day of Pentecost); (2) enablements through supernatural gifts of power (_pneumatic charismata_), see Rom. 1:11; 1 Cor. 12:6-11 NIV; and (3) grants of authority to establish the government of the Kingdom of Heaven (_domas_), see Eph. 4:11-12 NIV. Each administration of power has a distinct function to accomplish Christ's purposes through the individual and for the corporate Body.

Phaneros, the Holy Spirit's spontaneous administrations of power, is meant to change the environment into which Christ is actively inserting His purposes. For example, preceding the Day of Pentecost described in Acts chapter 2 was the execution of the Son of God through a collaboration of Jewish and Roman authorities, with the general populous' encouragement. Laying this accusation on the populous, Peter said:

> *Jesus of Nazareth was a man accredited by God to you by miracles, wonders and signs, which God did among you through Him, as you yourselves know. This man was handed over to you by God's set purpose and foreknowledge; and you, with the help of wicked men, put Him to death by nailing Him to the cross* (Acts 2:22b-23 NIV).

Peter's charge describes Jesus's execution as an extreme act of rejecting God. Crucifying Jesus demonstrated the people's depravity and departure from God—having become so entrenched in their hostilities as to ignore God's accreditation of Jesus.

These people were unlikely to receive any new initiatives from God unless God Himself changed the environment into which He was placing the corporate Son. God acted through spontaneous supernatural power, and the result was immediate change.[99] *Phaneros* gifts are spontaneous demonstrations of power that bring immediate change.

Pneumatic charismata are some of the longer-term effects of the baptism of the Spirit manifested consistently through the impartation of enablements:

> *To one there is given through the Spirit the message of wisdom, to another the message of knowledge by means of the same Spirit, to another faith by the same Spirit, to another gifts of healing by that one Spirit, to another miraculous powers, to another prophecy, to another distinguishing between spirits, to another speaking in different kinds of tongues, and to still another the interpretation of tongues. All these are the work of one and the same Spirit,*

and He gives them to each one, just as He determines (1 Corinthians 12:8-11 NIV).

These gifts relate to the way God meant to live through each person. This category of gifting is described as "gifts of helps"; and whereas an individual may possess extremely strong manifestations of some gifts, all the gifts in this category are available to each person at a level commensurate with their calling.

People often will exhibit an innate propensity for certain aspects of a gift, because it is part of who that person is meant to be or become. All believers possess one or more of these spiritual gifts. If any gift within this context is lacking in support of one's calling, one should "earnestly desire" that gift and should ask for an endowment of it.

It is important to distinguish between gifts of the Spirit and a person's calling. A calling is the destiny that God has assigned to each person. Whereas, a gift is the enablement of that calling.[100] The full expression and power of these gifts, however, cannot be expressed absent the baptism of the Spirit.

Pneumatic charismata are gifts of enablement, operating in different people differently. Each gift's function and expression through a person depends on that person's calling. For example, there are an array of styles and applications to the gift of prophecy. Some may have prophetic visions or dreams, while others have a word from the Lord. Still others may have insight through particular mediums, such as numerical emphases.

Adding further variety to each gift is that, apart from the form, the substance of each person's gift is unique to that person. Some may see the unfolding of future events; others may have words of personal prophecy; and still others may have the prophetic gift of interpreting the meaning of events. Both the form and the content are enablements of the individual's specific calling.

The third administration of the Holy Spirit is the distribution of gifts of government, or *domas*. While every person has a calling and receives the distribution of enablements for that calling, gifts of government are a much more limited distribution. The reason, simply, is that not everyone is called to function governmentally in one of these gifts.[101]

> *It was He who gave some to be apostles, some to be prophets, some to be evangelists, and some to be pastors and teachers, to prepare God's people for works of service, so that the body of Christ may be built up until we all reach unity in the faith and in the knowledge of the Son of God and become mature, attaining to the whole measure of the fullness of Christ* (Ephesians 4:11-13 NIV).

God has given the gifts to be apostles, prophets, evangelists, pastors, and teachers to establish the order of His Kingdom on the earth.

Although not all people are called to one of these gifts, governmentally, each of these gifts is meant to impart aspects of that gift to the whole Body of Christ. For example, contact with someone who is an apostle should impart an administration of order together with an expectation of receiving revelation of mysteries, which describes the apostolic gift but not the specific calling of any apostle. This impartation produces a mind-set of order consistent with the government of God in each person who receives it, allowing others to fit easily in their place in the Kingdom's order.

These *doma* gifts are for the "equipping of the saints," and the maturing of the Body of Christ.[102] The alternative to the proper functioning of these gifts is to be "infants, tossed back and forth by the waves, and blown here and there by every wind of teaching and by the cunning and craftiness of men in their deceitful scheming."[103]

The baptism of the Spirit introduces the believer to the supernatural reality of the power of God. When a person experiences the baptism of the Spirit, that person is transported from the natural world into some immediate contact with the reality of the Spirit—bringing forth these gifts.

Whereas *pneumatic charismata* are for the enabling of a person's destiny, *doma* gifts are for the proper functioning of the Kingdom of

God and the maturing of the Body of Christ. Each administration of Christ's power serves a specific purpose.[104]

Repentance and the Baptism of the Spirit

One cannot experience the power of the Holy Spirit significantly while the mind-set of a person's soul prevails, defining the person's reality. Gifts of the Spirit do not function independently of the Spirit of God. Thus, when a person's soul determines one's thoughts and actions in a certain area, it hinders the Spirit in leading the person through communion with that person's spirit. Therefore, to function fully in the gifts that result from this baptism, a person must engage the process for his or her spirit's dominance—that is, repentance from acts that lead to death.[105]

The soul helps translate the will of a person's spirit, governed entirely by the Spirit of God, into the natural world, but the soul cannot empower any action beyond that which a person is physically capable. The soul, supported by the orphan's culture into which each person is born, rejects the rule of the Holy Spirit and therefore fights with the human spirit for control over the person. When the soul is in control, all of the person's actions are focused on self-provision and protection, the imperatives of that default culture. The Holy Spirit is then unable to operate fully through that person. Therefore, while the baptism of the Spirit confers power, that power is enabled only when the human spirit is in fellowship with the Holy Spirit.

Where a person's mind is preoccupied with provision and protection, the person is limited in the resources to achieve those ends to his or her own ingenuity and craft. Scripture identifies this concept. God revealed it to Adam after the fall, saying, "By the sweat of your brow you will eat your food until you return to the ground, since from it you were taken; for dust you are and to dust you will return."[106] God was identifying mankind's condition when humans no longer saw themselves as spirit clothed in flesh, but only as the flesh that was made from dust. This changed the economy by which people lived; with their changed perception, their provision would only come from labor.

This was the natural consequence of mankind's loss of its identity as sons of God, operating only within the culture of the orphan, until Jesus restored mankind's original relationship to God.

When a person represents God as a son, the resources of His Kingdom and the economy of the Spirit are available to achieve the purposes for the person's representation.[107] When the Spirit imparts the power of Christ to a person, the person becomes able to function as a son of God. But, it is impossible for someone to represent God utilizing the strength of one's soul, because the soul cannot adequately define or support the purposes for one's sonship.[108]

Repentance and the renewing of the mind is a necessary foundation for the activities of the Spirit in the life of a believer. The change of mind-sets, from orphan to son, results also in a change of purpose. When a person no longer sees himself as fatherless, the Spirit may work to free him from an orphan's imperatives, and he can take up representation of his Father. Otherwise, the Holy Spirit will resist the use of His power through the person—though the person remains saved, there will be a pervasive state of powerlessness leaving one susceptible to the enemy's attacks. The baptism of the Spirit confers all of the requisite empowerment to represent the Father and to radiate His glory.

The Baptism of the Spirit and Sonship

Typically, a fundamentally different view of one's identity accompanies this baptism of power with the Spirit. Because spiritual gifts follow one's calling, the person becomes aware of the basis for his or her calling: that the person has changed from being a servant to becoming a son. The calling of a son is to represent the interests of the Father in the earth.

One who has experienced the baptism of the Spirit but who continues to harbor the orphan or servant mind-set may desire to utilize spiritual gifts in furtherance of personal goals. The servant mind-set seeks to please God through some work, and the person mistakenly will believe that spiritual gifts are either tools to serve these goals or a reward for good performance. This mistake comes from an erroneous view of mankind's relationship to God. Whereas the servant believes in a *quid pro quo* ("something for something [else]") relationship, God created people and placed them in the earth as His sons for the specific purpose of showing His invisible qualities.

The Spirit of God does not typically function to empower an individual's own choices and plans. The Spirit may show the goodness of God to others through one who has not yet changed from that default orphan culture, but eventually, the individual must decide to change or face the inevitable consequences of choosing to serve his or her personal interests—usually the decline of power and calling, and, potentially, exposure as one who is serving personal interests. If the person is unaware of the mind-set fueling the self-provision and protection that would attempt to usurp spiritual gifts for personal use, the result often is the person's frustration or doubt that spiritual gifts are real.

This is one area in which a spiritual father can help identify the cause of frustration and help the person overcome the default orphan culture motivating that person toward self-interests. A spiritual father helps one understand what it means to be a son to a loving father. The culture of a son that develops from this relationship will be supported by the Spirit. The house of God is built upon the love of the Father for the son and the inherent trust of the Father by the son, allowing the son to represent the Father's qualities in all things.

This order enables the gifts of the Spirit to function fully within an individual, because it instills the culture of a son and the representation of the Father in the person. Since a son is assured of his provision and protection by his Father, there is no need to try to manipulate the power and authority that results from the baptism of the Holy Spirit in furtherance of the basic survival imperatives. Jesus's instructions are to avoid such distractions:

> *Therefore I tell you, do not worry about your life, what you will eat or drink; or about your body, what you will wear. Is not life more important than food, and the body more*

important than clothes? Look at the birds of the air; they do not sow or reap or store away in barns, and yet your heavenly Father feeds them. Are you not much more valuable than they? Who of you by worrying can add a single hour to his life?

And why do you worry about clothes? See how the lilies of the field grow. They do not labor or spin. Yet I tell you that not even Solomon in all his splendor was dressed like one of these. If that is how God clothes the grass of the field, which is here today and tomorrow is thrown into the fire, will He not much more clothe you, O you of little faith? So do not worry, saying, "What shall we eat?" or "What shall we drink?" or "What shall we wear?" For the pagans run after all these things, and your heavenly Father knows that you need them. But seek first His kingdom and His righteousness, and all these things will be given to you as well (Matthew 6:25-33 NIV).

The baptism of the Spirit is a baptism designed to empower mankind's original purpose, displaying the goodness of God the Father uniquely through the individual and fully through the corporate Body of Christ.

Baptism by the Spirit

For we were all baptized by one Spirit into one body—whether Jews or Greeks, slave or free—and we were all given the one Spirit to drink (1 Corinthians 12:13 NIV).

The Holy Spirit integrates the newly born-again person into the Body of Christ as a unique part of the Body. Being fit into the Body changes the person's identity from one defined by talents, occupation, or accomplishments, to one whom God defined uniquely for that person before he or she was born, and an identity that, when revealed fully, will perfectly display an aspect of God's character.[109]

The Body of Christ is a reference to the corporate Son whose purpose is to completely display the fullness of God in the earth. The baptism by the Spirit is one of the Holy Spirit's tasks, by which He assembles people into the Body of Christ according to God's original intent both for the corporate Son and for each individual comprised within it. The Holy Spirit is familiar with God's original intent for the creation of every person:

> *"No eye has seen, no ear has heard, no mind has conceived what God has prepared for those who love Him"—but God has revealed it to us by His Spirit. The Spirit searches all things, even the deep things of God. For who among men knows the thoughts of a man except the man's spirit within him? In the same way no one knows the thoughts of God except the Spirit of God* (1 Corinthians 2:9b-11 NIV).

Through the baptism by the Spirit, a person becomes "fitly joined" to the corporate Christ.[110]

This baptism is integral to the process that reveals the believer's calling, empowerment, and way of life as a son of God. When one is born again, the Holy Spirit works to restore that person's spirit to preeminence over the person's soul, so that the influence of the spirit replaces that of the person's soul in governing the person's thoughts and actions.[111] This process reconnects the spirit of man to the Spirit of God and restores access to the mind of God, enabling the person to engage this new way of life.[112] The person is born again to be made a son of God:

> *And if the Spirit of Him who raised Jesus from the dead is living in you, He who raised Christ from the dead will also give life to your mortal bodies through His Spirit, who lives in you. …because those who are led by the Spirit of God are sons of God. For you did not receive a spirit that makes you a slave again to fear, but you received the Spirit*

of sonship. And by Him we cry, "Abba, Father." The Spirit Himself testifies with our spirit that we are God's children (Romans 8:11,14-16 NIV).

And Jesus taught, "...no one can enter the kingdom of God unless he is born of water and the Spirit. Flesh gives birth to flesh, but the Spirit gives birth to spirit. You should not be surprised at My saying, 'You must be born again.'"[113] Each one who is born again of the Spirit walks in the empowerment of the Spirit individually, and is assembled by the Holy Spirit into an orderly functioning corporate entity.

This baptism occurs at the same time the Holy Spirit enters a person. The individual is then assembled as part of the corporate expression of God now available in the world: the Body of Christ.

The Body of Christ is a spiritual entity composed of human spirits, assembled by the Holy Spirit into one corporate whole. Jesus once presented this whole on the earth in the body of one man. His was an accurate and exact representation of the character of God. Jesus was the "Anointed One" because the Spirit within Him was unique. Although every human being has a spirit that is capable of putting some aspect of God on display, Jesus was given the role of fully representing the nature of God.[114] The spirit that existed within the man Jesus that is capable of this function is known as the Christ. Upon Jesus's resurrection, the spirit of Christ began to receive and assemble all spirits returning to God into one corporate whole, continuing Jesus's work on the earth.

No one alone can continue this work. Christ works through all the bodies of persons whose spirits have been assembled into this one spirit. Paul emphasized the functioning of the corporate man as the accurate representation of God's divine nature:

> *The body is a unit, though it is made up of many parts; and though all its parts are many, they form one body. So it is with Christ. ... Now the body is not made up of one part but of many. ... As it is, there are many parts, but one*

> *body. ... Now you are the body of Christ, and each one of you is a part of it* (1 Corinthians 12:12,14,20,27 NIV).

Each part is important, but the fullness of Christ is presented again in the earth only through the corporate functioning.

Some have overemphasized the individual parts of the Body and the impact of their functions. Assigning such importance to an individual or a certain gift is common, because to some, this practice provides guidance for how each person should live his or her life, being detached from the relationships within the Body. This emphasis has led to a religious culture that has established a hierarchy of values assigned to spiritual gifts. The result is arbitrarily exalted statuses of persons who practice certain gifts, and entire ministries have been formed largely around leaders functioning expertly in certain highly valued *pneumatic charismata*.

However, the image of the corporate Son as a Body with many parts should define the emphasis of how all believers are meant to relate to one another. No part of a human body defines any particular calling attributed to the whole, no matter how effectively it functions. Similarly, the purpose of the whole Body of Christ is not attributed to or expressed entirely by the functioning of individual parts. The parts are incapable, by themselves, of exactly representing the divine nature of God in a manner after Jesus's example or in the continuing corporate expression in the Body of Christ. While it is necessary that the parts function well, only their assembled state contains the continuation of the work of Christ.

The baptism by the Spirit takes a person whose identity was defined by his or her own actions; translates them into the Body of Christ, giving that person an identity that is the full expression of who that person is made to be; and gives further depth to that person's relationship to God as Father. Commonly, this change is inconsistent with one's present way of life. The change of one's identity not only requires a changed mind-set, but often a change of lifestyle as well. The laying down of one's identity and purpose in order to accommodate God's will is "a living sacrifice."[115]

The challenges to one's present circumstances that require change may be helpfully discerned by a spiritual father. When one is born again, he is born into the family of God as a son. However, the culture of his soul is still intact, and although he has been spiritually reconciled, he naturally understands the relationship through the culture of an orphan. He has been repatriated to God the Father and has access to the resources of the great House of God. Yet he still views himself through the filters of his native culture.

In order for him to transition to the culture of a son, he must be tutored and disciplined in the culture of Heaven. This task is assigned to a spiritual father.[116] A father who loves in this way can help identify the time for such change and support the individual through the inevitable challenges.

Baptism of Fire (Suffering)

Christ, the "author and perfecter of our faith" (see Heb. 12:2 NIV), administers the refining fire of discipline and suffering to produce sons of God who are fit to represent their Father.[117] Suffering refines the believer in specific ways, which are necessary for the person to mature.

Specifically, this baptism helps to transfer control of the person from the soul to the spirit. Suffering exposes the soul's vulnerability and shatters the false perception of control over the person's life. Suffering is experienced when the soul perceives that its view of reality is shifting from a basis of reason to one of revelation. The soul may control the process of reason and the decisions that come from it, but it is incapable of influencing the substance of revelation. The corresponding vulnerability makes the human feel adrift and at the mercy of the unknown. This loss of control is one of the human's greatest fears, but it is necessary to allow one's spirit to part the veil of the apparent loss of control and return to the reality of the spirit and the provision and protection of the Kingdom of God.[118] Exposing the soul elevates the mind-set of one's spirit over the person and further establishes the individual as a son of God, since a son is defined as one with whose spirit the Holy Spirit fellowships.[119]

In wresting away the soul's strongholds over various areas of one's life, the baptism of fire produces a critical transition toward raising mature sons.

> *My son, do not make light of the Lord's discipline, and do not lose heart when He rebukes you, because the Lord disciplines those He loves, and He punishes everyone He accepts as a son. Endure hardship as discipline; God is treating you as sons. For what son is not disciplined by his father? If you are not disciplined (and everyone undergoes discipline), then you are illegitimate children and not true sons* (Hebrews 12:5b-8 NIV, quotation marks omitted).

"[T]hose who are led by the Spirit of God are *sons* [*huios*] of God (emphasis added)."[120] The baptism of fire is critical to the process of being led by the Spirit, and therefore, becoming a mature son who can represent the Father.

To be led by the Spirit, a person must be saved from the reality created when Adam first sinned, separating himself from God. This separation awakened the soul of man, which is the seat of man's independence from God.[121]

When the eyes of the soul were opened, man's view of himself and his purpose in creation underwent a complete change. He transitioned from being a son to becoming fatherless; and in that transition, he lost the vision of himself as being spirit, like his Father, and saw himself as flesh.[122]

Every person must be saved from the dominance of the soul, which conflicts with being led by the Spirit. Christ accomplishes this saving of the soul through suffering and discipline—the baptism of fire. A believer cannot reach the maturity by which he or she is capable of, representing the Father exactly, without suffering that is discipline.[123]

The baptism of fire is an area of every believer's life in which he or she will need help through the trials. There is an order that God has given that allows every believer to grow through suffering. A spiritual father is key to help interpret a person's trials and sufferings and provide an anchor for the person, keeping the person focused on Christ's purpose for this particular time in his or her life and keeping the person from being completely overwhelmed by this process of refinement.

The baptism of fire is not a singular event in the life of a believer but occurs numerous times throughout the stages of one's maturity. It is administered on an individual basis depending on individual circumstances. The kind, intensity, and duration depend on the individual's present state and calling as a son of God. "No discipline seems pleasant at the time, but painful. Later on, however, it produces a harvest of righteousness and peace for those who have been trained by it."[124] Progressive suffering, administered by Christ, is consistent with the degree of change required in each stage of a believer's life.

Even Jesus learned obedience through suffering. "Although He was a son, He learned obedience from what He suffered and, once made perfect, He became the source of eternal salvation for all who obey Him and was designated by God to be high priest in the order of Melchizedek."[125] This time of perfection took place during the eighteen years of Jesus's life mostly unaccounted for in Scripture—from His beginning of being about His Father's business as a child, during which time "Jesus increased in wisdom and stature, and in favour with God and man," leading up to His presentation to the world as the Son of God.[126] The time of Jesus's preparation shows both the methodology (suffering) and the goal (increased wisdom, stature, and favor with God and man) of the baptism of fire. The baptism of fire is inseparable from the process of growing to maturity. The more mature one becomes, the greater the wisdom and insight that the Spirit of God imparts to the individual. One cannot assume the responsibilities of an ambassador for the Kingdom of God unless that person has been prepared for that role. Peter taught,

> *Dear friends, do not be surprised at the painful trial you are suffering, as though something strange were happening*

to you. But rejoice that you participate in the sufferings of Christ, so that you may be overjoyed when His glory is revealed. If you are insulted because of the name of Christ, you are blessed, for the Spirit of glory and of God rests on you. If you suffer, it should not be as a murderer or thief or any other kind of criminal, or even as a meddler. However, if you suffer as a Christian, do not be ashamed, but praise God that you bear that name (1 Peter 4:12-16 NIV).

Before one may be put on display as a mature son, that person will become repetitively familiar with suffering.

These baptisms form a necessary process in maturing the sons of God: To represent the Father, one must be born again (a process beginning in the act of repentance, and symbolized in part through water baptism); one must be empowered with the Holy Spirit so that Christ may live through that person (accomplished by Christ through the baptism of the Spirit); one must be accurately positioned in the Body of Christ (accomplished by the Holy Spirit through the baptism by the Spirit); and one must be led by the Spirit (accomplished by Christ through the baptism of fire). These baptisms or their effects are, in some ways, automatic administrations in the life of a believer.

As long as one chooses Christ, and is able to continually repent and renew his mind, the person is not only a son of God, but God also will be steadfast in equipping the person, giving him or her a place as a son of God, and undertaking the necessary training to mature the person through the stages of maturity for a son.

There are, however, other administrations in the House of God put in place both for the proper functioning of the House and for the maturing of its sons. *The Laying On of Hands* translates the stages of maturity into a familial setting. Not only does the name of the doctrine imply close, intimate relationships, but its function is necessary for the speed and development of a culture that belongs to the family of God.

CHAPTER FOUR

THE LAYING ON OF HANDS

A Messenger People

> *How, then, can they call on the one they have not believed in? And how can they believe in the one of whom they have not heard? And how can they hear without someone preaching to them? And how can they preach unless they are sent? As it is written, "How beautiful are the feet of those who bring good news!" ... Faith comes from hearing the message, and the message is heard through the word of Christ* (Romans 10:14-15,17 NIV).

It may seem odd that the laying on of hands is an Elementary Doctrine. For most, the laying on of hands has become an antiquated gesture, an archaic tradition, or a purely ceremonial practice without a readily apparent purpose. It is a lost doctrine; and therefore, the majority of believers today have not been taught, and do not practice, one of the fundamental principles for "go[ing] on to maturity."[127]

The nature of religion's structural order is responsible for the doctrine's present neglect. The laying on of hands relates intricately to the authority and power of God's Kingdom. In institutions where authority and power are derived from the people, the laying on of hands has become irrelevant or unnecessary.

Traditional religious order places the leaders as representatives of the people, offering sacrifices to God on the people's behalf. This is the classic order of priests.[128] Over time, religious groups have structured their own governance around the characteristics of secular governmental order. The consent of the members is the basis for modern church order.

The Roman emperor Constantine introduced this form of church order when he made Christianity the Roman Empire's official religion. Within the Empire, the authority of the church shifted formally from the empowerment of the Holy Spirit to empowerment by the Roman republic. As a state functionary, the church received the favor of the state while producing a citizenry loyal to the government. Being a church member was part of the bundle of civil rights to which the citizen of the state became entitled.

Modern churches tend to epitomize a democratic order, where members possess an underlying assumption that it is their right to determine the governmental structure of the church. By making the church an agent of the state, Constantine elevated the power of the state over that of the church, and the rights of a citizen defined both participation in the state and in the church.

In countries where there is an official state church, all civil rights transfer in whole to a citizen's church membership, and the state church may not deny the rights of citizens who are also church members. This framework of church governance has made its way into churches that are independent of the state, because the basis of authority is derived from the consent of the citizens who are also church members.

Whether raised by the state or by the people, the role of leaders as representatives of the people has further required that they be empowered by the people. The pastors and priests function as the representatives of the people to God and not as God's representatives to the people, inasmuch as their authority does not come from God, but from the people.[129]

Modern institutions, in many ways, have derived from the Levitical order of priests. In doing so, they have ignored the order and authority of the New Testament Church, derived not from the Levitical priesthood, but from the order of Melchizedek.[130]

Both the high priest and the entire order of Melchizedek are established by God's decree, not by the consent of the people. In the New Testament Church, Christ is the High Priest, forever, in the order of Melchizedek.[131] This priesthood supersedes the previous Levitical order and has rendered it obsolete:

> *If perfection could have been attained through the Levitical priesthood (for on the basis of it the law was given to the people), why was there still need for another priest to come—one in the order of Melchizedek, not in the order of Aaron? For when there is a change of the priesthood, there must also be a change of the law* (Hebrews 7:11-12 NIV; see also Hebrews 8:13 NIV).

Christ is the only representative of mankind to God, because He is all that is necessary:

> *Because Jesus lives forever, He has a permanent priesthood. Therefore He is able to save completely those who come to God through Him, because He always lives to intercede for them. Such a high priest meets our need—one who is holy, blameless, pure, set apart from sinners, exalted above the heavens. Unlike the other high priests, He does not need to offer sacrifices day after day, first for His own sins, and then for the sins of the people. He sacrificed for their sins once for all when He offered Himself* (Hebrews 7:24-27 NIV).

With the change of priesthood, Christ also administers a return to God's original intent for His relationship to mankind.

When God created man, He empowered mankind to act as God's representative. Adam was given authority by God to rule the creation, and God appeared vicariously through him. Adam was the chief priest of the covenant by which God ruled creation. As God's vicar, he was the ruler over all creation. Adam was the king of the earth, a royal priest.

The original covenant was that which created the order of royal priests; kings of righteousness and princes of peace. *Melchi-* (king) *-zedek* (righteousness) is the priesthood that administrated the original covenant. Although Adam became disobedient, this order continued until it was changed at Mount Sinai, when God introduced a covenant with Israel.[132]

At the cross, however, the order of Levi came to an end, and the order of Melchizedek was reintroduced. In Christ, all the priests of this order would represent God to the people:

> *The ministry Jesus has received is as superior to theirs as the covenant of which He is mediator is superior to the old one, and it is founded on better promises. … This is the covenant I will make with the house of Israel after that time, declares the Lord. I will put My laws in their minds and write them on their hearts. I will be their God, and they will be My people. … By calling this covenant "new," He has made the first one obsolete; and what is obsolete and aging will soon disappear* (Hebrews 8:6,10,13 NIV).

In the New Testament, the people come to God through Christ. He is their High Priest, and they are God's people. And, God's people are messengers.

It is the authority of Christ in the New Testament Church that gave rise to the *apostolos*, the messengers of God. The term *apostle* means "sent ones" or "messengers."[133] The early apostles understood that they were messengers of Christ, sent with the authority to represent Him.

The term *apostolos* is synonymous with the term *angelos*.[134] Of these messengers, *angelos* or *apostolos,* there are those that ascend and those that descend, meaning some originate in Heaven and some originate on the earth. Jesus spoke to Nathanael about angels "ascending and descending."[135] The messengers that originate in Heaven are different messengers from those who originate on the earth.

The messengers who originate in Heaven are angels.[136] These messengers come from Heaven to bring a word from God to the earth, and then they return to God. These are spirit beings who normally reside in Heaven from whence they are dispatched. These angels are never involved in the administration of the message, and therefore never lay hands upon humans for the impartation of the administration of the message, though they are resisted by the enemy for the messages they carry.[137]

The messengers who originate in the earth are people. These *angelus* may also ascend and descend by being invited into Heaven to witness great happenings and to bring back a message.[138]

John was the messenger summoned to Heaven to see what God was unveiling. Similarly, Paul speaks of himself as being "caught up to the third heaven."[139] The message these *angelos* or *apostolos* carry does not originate with them. In ordinary Greek, the term *apostolos* means "post man" or, colloquially, "mail man." But, these messengers are also God's people, representing Him to the earth. Christ prepares them carefully so that they are capable of delivering the message and participating in its administration.

> *Surely you have heard about the administration of God's grace that was given to me for you, that is, the mystery made known to me by revelation, as I have already written briefly. In reading this, then, you will be able to understand my insight into the mystery of Christ, which was not made known to men in other generations as it has now been revealed by the Spirit to God's holy apostles and prophets. ... Although I am less than the least of all God's people, this grace was given me: to preach to the Gentiles*

> *the unsearchable riches of Christ, and to make plain to everyone the administration of this mystery, which for ages past was kept hidden in God, who created all things* (Ephesians 3:2-5,8-9 NIV).

The apostle and the message are meant to be the two components of the same gift. They are, therefore, given both the message and the administration.

The laying on of hands is a crucial part of the administration that causes the message from Heaven to be imparted from those to whom it is given to those for whom it is intended, who benefit from it. When God releases a message from Heaven, it is the message itself that changes the earth. The administration through the laying on of hands builds the Body of Christ together through the message from Heaven.

> *Consequently, you are no longer foreigners and aliens, but fellow citizens with God's people and members of God's household, built on the foundation of the apostles and prophets, with Christ Jesus Himself as the chief cornerstone. In Him the whole building is joined together and rises to become a holy temple in the Lord. And in Him you too are being built together to become a dwelling in which God lives by His Spirit* (Ephesians 2:19-22 NIV).

This impartation is designed to convey the reality of the message with the grace to establish this word through those who have been commissioned and sent by this process. The reality of the Kingdom of God is meant to pass from one person to another with an exponential multiplication of the effect of the message.

The reason that the messengers, human or angelic, are routinely resisted by the demonic is that the demonic understands that the message itself changes things on the earth. When the message comes, together with the messengers, it has the effect of illuminating the darkness of error and deception. Hidden things are suddenly disclosed; long hidden truth emerges and may be seen by whoever desires the truth.

In the light of that revelation, the deceiver's craft is plainly seen and the foundation of his house of lies is permanently damaged. People are set free to pursue the path of truth, and only those who thrive in an environment of deceit long for and remain in the darkness. The message itself brings power and authority and must be administered by a messenger prepared and established by the authority of Christ, the Head and High Priest.

The priests of this order are God's people, His messengers. Christ prepares the messengers before sending them out. He establishes them with His authority amongst those to whom He sends them. And, the message they carry is one of the power and authority of the Kingdom that binds together the House of God. The laying on of hands is necessary for order, because it presents the message in the form of His grace and goodness through God's people, as was His original intent in creating mankind.

The doctrine of the laying of on hands has four major applications: (1) healing, typically of physical diseases and mental disorders; (2) impartation; (3) confirmation of gifts and callings; and (4) commissioning and sending. The laying on of hands represents the primary way in which the anointing, authority, and order of the Kingdom of God is expanded person to person. Each of these applications represents a different aspect of this order—though they are altogether integrated: the laying on of hands reveals one's anointing and spreads that anointing to others; it confirms a person's gifts; and it is the process for commissioning a person according to his or her calling in Christ.

Healing

Healing by the laying on of hands is a demonstration of power with two purposes: (1) The demonstration identifies the one laying hands on another as a messenger sent from God, and (2) it establishes the authority of the Kingdom the messenger represents in the circumstances into which he or she is sent. These dual purposes identify the anointing of a messenger directly to the people and expand the authority of God's Kingdom, through His messenger, for their benefit.

God has always spread His Kingdom through messengers. He created Adam to extend the Kingdom of Heaven to the earth.[140] He sent Jesus Christ to reconcile mankind to this original purpose.[141] And, when Christ returned to Heaven, His Body, made up of His people, have continued Christ's work in the earth.[142]

The early Church continued this practice, in which anointed messengers were trained, commissioned, and sent to spread the Gospel of the Kingdom. Each of these examples shows God's dedication to spreading His Kingdom on the earth through His messengers.

The first purpose for healing by the laying on of hands is to demonstrate a messenger's anointing, so that the ones witnessing the demonstration can receive the message. For this reason, the more common practice in Scripture for healing physical or mental illnesses is by the laying on of hands—though the Lord may accomplish healing without physical contact.[143]

During His ministry, Jesus commonly demonstrated His divine mandate by the laying on of hands for the purpose of healing.[144] Similarly, the early apostles' message was regularly attended by the laying on of hands for healing.[145] The messenger extends God's goodness and mercy to the one being healed while the power of the Spirit establishes the messenger's credibility.[146]

The second purpose for healing by the laying on of hands is to establish the superiority of God's Kingdom over its opposition. Anytime a messenger is sent in the name of the Lord to establish the Kingdom's authority, the messenger is sent with the full expectation of opposition. The Lord equips and prepares the messenger accordingly. The message is not just words, but the demonstration of power and the authority of the Kingdom to accomplish change.[147] By clarifying the messenger's anointing, the act of healing, as a miraculous sign performed among the people, establishes the messenger's authority to engage the enemy among the people.

God's messengers are made credible among the people and established as figures with authority and power to oppose the kingdom of darkness' strongholds that resist the spread of God's Kingdom. Not limited to the practice of laying hands on another, there are numerous examples throughout the New Testament of the works of the messengers who are established further by miraculous signs. In the great commissioning of His disciples, Jesus Christ assured them of the signs and wonders that would attest to their message:

> *And these signs will accompany those who believe: In My name they will drive out demons; they will speak in new tongues; they will pick up snakes with their hands; and when they drink deadly poison, it will not hurt them at all; they will place their hands on sick people, and they will get well* (Mark 16:17-18 NIV).

Paul wrote, "For we know, brothers loved by God, that He has chosen you, because our gospel came to you not simply with words, but also with power, with the Holy Spirit and with deep conviction. You know how we lived among you for your sake."[148] The miraculous attended those sent, for their benefit and for the benefit of those to whom they preached the Gospel. Thus, the message was spread person to person accompanied through the laying on of hands, establishing the message and the messenger with power and authority.

A Kingdom of Power

Jesus's detractors argued that His displays of power must have been empowered by Satan, specifically concerning His command over demons. Responding, Jesus revealed one of the great truths of the Kingdom of God, saying, "If I cast out demons by the Spirit of God then the Kingdom of Heaven has come to you."[149]

The heavenly and earthly realms operate according to orders of power and authority, in which the Kingdom of Heaven is the seat of the highest order. It is through Christ and His emissaries and such demonstrations of power that the Kingdom extends into the earth.

The Elementary Doctrines

The Kingdom of God is a kingdom of power. When Christ sends one of its representatives to an area or a people, the purpose is to establish the Kingdom's authority. Establishing the Kingdom's authority allows the messenger to operate in power and elicit change, overcoming the opposition to the Kingdom, as light brought into a dark place.

The laying on of hands is the most basic practice for accrediting God's messengers, giving them the proper weight of authority through signs and wonders. Therefore, the laying on of hands is also fundamental to engaging the enemy with power and authority.

This doctrine's loss has contributed directly to the current powerlessness of the Church. Leaders are not required to demonstrate that they are operating out of an anointing from God, and their message has devolved from one of a Kingdom that triumphs over its enemies to social and historical messages, designed for easy consumption. Believers in the present church system are encouraged to see God through their historic and national cultures, or they are exposed routinely to a message designed to spur them to greater levels of activity motivated by their souls.

God has always intended to present the message of His Kingdom through messengers. Messengers are accredited by the anointing from the Holy Spirit. This anointing is demonstrably evinced by the person's way of life—displaying God's goodness—and through the demonstration of authority over the kingdom of darkness.

Delivering the message in this way yields dramatically different results.

Shortly after the Day of Pentecost, Peter and John healed a crippled man at the gates of the temple, and their actions became a direct challenge to the religious authorities, because Peter and John claimed to have healed the man as messengers sent by Christ.[150]

They were swiftly arrested and sternly warned to stop performing miraculous signs and invoking Christ's authority.

Because they and others frequently persisted, the gap between the two sides widened and eventually resulted in full-scale persecution of the early believers. The believers survived and thrived during this persecution because they received the message with power and authority of the Kingdom of God, demonstrating the effect of overcoming opposition to the Kingdom through power.[151]

The message is reliably conveyed when supported by a demonstration of power. One example of this principle is when Jesus healed a blind man in the Book of John, chapter 9.

After his miraculous healing by the laying on of Jesus's hands, religious authorities rigorously questioned the man, who had been blind from birth. They tried to discredit Jesus on theological grounds, because He had healed the man on the Sabbath.

The man did not have the training to debate with them successfully, but understood that Jesus represented divine authority, given the undeniable evidence of his own healing. The man was not dissuaded by the questions of the religious authorities even though he could not offer them a theological answer. His faith in Jesus was anchored in his experience. His answers, therefore, were succinct and formidable. He declared simply, "One thing I do know. I was blind but now I see!" His experience similarly demonstrates how healing by the laying on of hands establishes the message and the authority of the Kingdom in the realms of opposition.

Those who rely upon the message of the Kingdom must be introduced to the Kingdom by an unimpeachable demonstration of authority and power. Paul wrote, "My message and my preaching were not with wise and persuasive words, but with a demonstration of the Spirit's power, so that your faith might not rest on men's wisdom, but on God's power."[152] The message of the Kingdom is one of God accrediting Jesus as the pattern Son, given rule over principalities and powers:

> *He raised Him from the dead and seated Him at His right hand in the heavenly realms, far above all rule and authority, power and dominion, and every title that can be given, not only in the present age but also in the one to come. And God placed all things under His feet and ap-*

pointed Him to be head over everything for the church (Ephesians 1:20b-22 NIV).

God established Jesus as the chosen Son through the signs and wonders that He demonstrated among the people.[153] God also raised Him from the dead, leaving no doubt that Jesus was anointed of God and that He was given all authority in Heaven and on earth as the basis for His Kingdom.

The message itself requires the establishing of power and authority.

For what I received I passed on to you as of first importance: that Christ died for our sins according to the Scriptures, that He was buried, that He was raised on the third day according to the Scriptures, and that He appeared to Peter, and then to the Twelve. ... For if the dead are not raised, then Christ has not been raised either. And if Christ has not been raised, your faith is futile; you are still in your sins (1 Corinthians 15:3-5,16-17 NIV).

God intends, for those who would place their lives under His authority and believe, that they be anchored in their belief either through experiencing or through witnessing the power of the Kingdom, from the beginning. Absent this anchor, modern believers are often easily swayed by intellectual arguments against the foundations of faith and hope, since they have neither seen nor experienced the authority and power of Christ.[154]

Church leaders' lack of experience with demonstrations of divine power has contributed directly to believers' weakness in the churches today. The Gospel with which the typical churchgoer is familiar is purely an intellectual gospel—reasoned discourse often reduced to altruistic statements—devoid of demonstrations of power.

One of the reasons people view this current gospel with skepticism is that typically it is delivered empty of demonstrations of miraculous power. God's divine presence is supposed to accompany the message of His goodness. The experience becomes the point of reference that holds faith in place until the Spirit of God can impart the mysteries of Heaven to someone who has matured. Separating the Gospel from its delivery by power and the Holy Spirit changes the message.

Many leaders have not been taught the Elementary Doctrine of the laying on of hands to demonstrate the miraculous power of God, as a way of showing His goodness to people in need. As a result, nothing authenticates the legitimacy of those who claim to preach the Good News of a Kingdom and who claim power and authority from the throne of God. The doctrine of laying hands on another has been lost largely because it recognizes that this Kingdom is a kingdom in which miraculous demonstrations of power are standard.

Yet Jesus and the early apostles laid the foundation of purpose for the laying on of hands for healing, and it became an integral part of daily life in the early Church.[155]

The laying on of hands for healing is an expression of power guided by the goodness of God and purposed to accredit the one through whom the Spirit accomplishes the healing.

Impartation

The transferring of gifts of the Spirit from one person to another occurs by the laying on of hands. This process is called impartation.

The scope and purpose of impartation distinguishes this aspect of the laying on of hands from the act of healing. Certainly, one aspect of what may be imparted to another through the laying on of hands is healing.[156] However, impartation through the laying on of hands is more broadly defined as the means of conveying the delegated power and authority of Christ for specific purposes. These purposes take various forms, but generally, may be described as establishing order and empowering the Body of Christ.

For example, the routine administration associated with the baptism of the Spirit is the laying on of hands.[157] However, there is no specific methodology required for the baptism of the Spirit, because Jesus Himself baptizes with the Holy Spirit.[158]

Among the variety of ways in which one may be baptized in the Spirit, laying on of hands administrates the baptism person to person, furthering the Kingdom of God through its messengers.

Impartation is one of the administrations permitted by the Holy Spirit for the authentication of gifts of government (*domas*) and the distribution of enablements (*pneumatic charismata*).[159]

A person laying hands on another is purporting to represent the Lord. His credibility to function in that capacity should already be established, but when the person is sent to a different area or people, he must be authenticated to that people and be established in the authority the person represents.

As discussed with the specific instances of healing, the laying on of hands accredits the messenger to the people and establishes that person's authority to operate in the capacity in which he or she is sent.

Where one is sent to impart aspects of the Holy Spirit, the recipients of the laying on of hands may rely upon the messenger's credibility. One being authenticated by laying on of hands and imparting some aspect of the Holy Spirit to another implies that the Spirit has accredited the person to function in the very thing he imparts. The requirement of accreditation also implies that laying on of hands must be consensual between the administrator of grace and the recipient.

The substance of what is imparted—for example, gifts of the Spirit—is different from the administrative process by which it is imparted. The gifts that are imparted may consist of those things that the Spirit has established in a person following the baptism of the Holy Spirit. The impartations may include gifts of helps, and depending on one's calling, gifts of governments as well. Supernatural gifts are necessary for the Body of Christ's orderly and effective functioning.

Everyone is endowed from birth with certain spiritual gifts, which become activated when he or she is baptized with the Spirit. Paul claimed a gift given to him from his birth, and that gift was confirmed after his encounter with Jesus on the road to Damascus, by Jesus Himself.[160] Other gifts are supplied as they are needed:

> *To one there is given through the Spirit the message of wisdom, to another the message of knowledge by means of the same Spirit, to another faith by the same Spirit, to another gifts of healing by that one Spirit, to another miraculous powers, to another prophecy, to another distinguishing between spirits, to another speaking in different kinds of tongues, and to still another the interpretation of tongues. ... Are all apostles? Are all prophets? Are all teachers? Do all work miracles? Do all have gifts of healing? Do all speak in tongues? Do all interpret? But eagerly desire the greater gifts. And now I will show you the most excellent way* (1 Corinthians 12:8-10,29-31 NIV).

The gifts that are necessary for some but not inherent may be supplied through the administration of impartation.[161]

The substance of impartation by the laying on of hands both furthers and is facilitated by the order of God's house. Paul's letters to the Romans and Corinthians, as a spiritual father to those believers, show how impartation is a part of this order.

In Corinth, there were others, such as Apollo and Peter, who served the Body of Christ, but Paul had a fatherly responsibility for them. Part of his duty was to ensure that they were properly equipped to function individually and corporately. Considering their condition, he was keenly aware of their need for greater wisdom and a keener sensitivity to the spirit of prophecy.[162]

Similarly, Paul was intimately aware of the hardship of the believers in Rome, and he longed to visit them in part to supply spiritual gifts to them: "I long to see you so that I may impart to you some spiritual gift to make you strong—that is, that you and I may be mutually encouraged by each other's faith."[163] As a spiritual father watching over a portion of his family, Paul knew what gifts were necessary for the effective functioning of that part of his family.

One of the active duties of a spiritual father is to closely monitor the spiritual condition of those under his care. Where there are deficits that may be remedied by impartations through the laying on of hands, it is part of the administration undertaken for their care and supply. Being established as fundamental to this order, the practice of the impartation of gifts through the laying on of hands should be widely practiced throughout the Body of Christ, subject to the restrictions related to the credibility of the one who imparts and to the consent of the one who receives.[164]

Confirmation

Confirmation of one's gifts and calling traditionally occurred by the laying on of hands.[165]

Certain gifts of the Spirit are resident within a person "from his mother's womb," and a person's calling is irrevocably determined by God.[166] Confirmation of one's gifts, however, comes after a time when the individual has been functioning in his or her gifts to the extent that others can testify of the person's readiness to function in a broader sphere in these gifts.

When believers reach the place of maturity, confirmation of that maturity and of the gifts that support their work is accomplished through the laying on of hands. Timothy provides an example of this process in the New Testament Church.

Timothy was called, together with Paul, to carry the word of the Lord among the Gentiles. His specific gift was that of being an apostle.[167] When the time came for his gifts to be confirmed, the leaders in two cities (Lystra and Iconium) attested to Timothy's faithfulness, because he had learned and become proficient in his gifts and gained an excellent reputation among the believers there.[168] He had reached such a level of competence in his functioning that he was recommended to join Paul's company. And because Paul and the elders of those cities knew Timothy, they confirmed the gift in Timothy through the laying on of hands.[169]

When Timothy was tested, his authentication to function had already been established, and Paul could encourage him by reminding Timothy of his confirmation.[170]

Another facet of this confirmation practice was to establish the believers who had come out of the pagan world into the Kingdom of God through the laying on of hands.[171] This is also another example of confirming one's gifts, because each person's calling, and therefore, inherent gifts, comes from one's identity in the Kingdom of God. This confirmation enables one to function in spiritual gifts, because the confirmation is established on the credibility of another.

In the Kingdom, no one has to make his or her own way or prove his right to function. The ones in authority make room for others to engage their functions, and when they have shown a level of maturity commensurate with their calling, they are confirmed in these places by those who have the authority to do so. Confirmation presumes that the person is operating in power and authority. This removes the need for self-authentication and provides continuity and expansion of service to the Body of Christ.

Today, confirmation has been reduced to a ceremony for the induction of a person into membership of religious groups. Biblical confirmation, however, is an act that recognizes the transformation of someone from the pagan culture to a son of God. It also establishes those who have been functioning in their gifts and callings at a level of maturity sufficient to be trustworthy and able to function in a wider sphere than before being confirmed.

Commissioning and Sending

In the New Testament, the pattern by which one was sent into ministry began with the person being confirmed in a particular gift and calling and was followed by a period of work within a certain location. After that, the Holy Spirit, through a prophetic utterance, would establish the person's readiness, commissioning him or her to be sent into a broader sphere of their calling. The sending would be undertaken by those in authority where the individual had worked and where he had become recognized in faithfulness. The leaders would recite their observation of the growth and maturity of the person as confirmation of his gifts and calling, and would then lay hands on that person and send him out from that location into the broader reaches of his destiny.

Paul and Timothy's journeys demonstrate this particular pattern.[172]

Paul had already possessed the gift of apostleship and was functioning in it for an entire year in the city of Antioch.[173] His functioning left no doubt of his readiness and reliability. The Holy Spirit ordained the occasion for the sending through a prophetic utterance:

> *While they were worshiping the Lord and fasting, the Holy Spirit said, "Set apart for me Barnabas and Saul for the work to which I have called them." So after they had fasted and prayed, they placed their hands on them and sent them off. The two of them, sent on their way by the Holy Spirit, went down to Seleucia and sailed from there to Cyprus* (Acts 13:2-4 NIV).

The company of elders, in agreement with the Holy Spirit and with one another, publicly placed their hands on Paul and Barnabas and sent them out to the work to which the Holy Spirit had called them. In this sending, they were accompanied by the Holy Spirit inasmuch as this was His orderly administration.

Timothy repeated the same pattern. Acts 16:1-2 tells the reader that Timothy was already functioning in his gift and calling in the cities of Lystra and Iconium before he was ready to accompany Paul, Silas, Luke, and others. The Holy Spirit spoke of his readiness through a prophetic utterance.[174] Then, the elders and Paul laid hands on him and commissioned him into his work and calling. Neither Paul nor Timothy sent themselves into their calling and ministries.

This orderly process contrasts starkly with the way people come forth in ministry today. In the New Testament Church, those in authority attested to the veracity of the prophetic word and joined in the commissioning process to release those being sent. The ones being sent were commissioned to function either in new locations or were given a wider increase of authority and scope of function consistent with their calling. In most of the historic churches, however, almost anyone who is a baptized member and meets other requirements, relating to marital status and other background and financial tests, may enroll in schools for formal training in the doctrines unique to that denomination.

Anyone who feels a call to ministry may initiate the process of entering ministry. This process typically involves first attending some form of Bible school training followed by an apprenticeship under the pastoral leadership of a congregation within that denomination. Upon completing a prescribed course of study, the person is assigned work within the organization, and careers are choreographed through the patterns common to that denomination.

Alternatively, one may pursue missionary work in some foreign destination, usually determined by one's ability to raise his or her own financial support and completion of outreach ministry training. These models do not recognize, foster, or support anyone's gifts or calling. Callings for "ordinary" members of the denomination are typically relegated to being financial supporters of the denomination and the ministries of those who lead.

The laying on of hands for commissioning and sending is a biblical pattern that stands on the order of God's House. In this pattern, those who are well-known for their reliable work are commissioned and sent to their callings. The ones commissioning and sending them are spiritual fathers who are themselves well-known for their godly character and reliable work of leading the House of God.

As involved fathers, they are able to recognize the gifts and callings of those under their care, and to nurture those gifts to maturity. This is a deliberate process that is personal in scope and application and knowledgeable of the ways of God. Those under such care will consistently transition to maturity and competent functionality. Their commissioning will occur as a matter of course. Whenever someone is ready to function among the believers in his or her calling, such a person is commissioned and sent by the laying on of hands.

The Elementary Doctrine of the laying on of hands has been largely neglected in present church administrations. As a result, believers are unaware of the central role of this doctrine spreading the Gospel of the Kingdom through qualified messengers. They do not understand the different purposes for the laying on of hands or how these expressions of the doctrine are interrelated.

The laying on of hands is the defining doctrine for extending the Kingdom of God into the earth through the people of God, His family.

CHAPTER FIVE
THE RESURRECTION OF THE DEAD

Death and resurrection are necessary for life in Christ. The next Elementary Doctrine, *The Resurrection of the Dead*, identifies someone as a new creation.

The prior life of a son of God does not aptly define him or her once the person is born again of the Spirit. A new creation replaces the old one, and a son of God exists where once a son of Adam lived.

God arranged the resurrection of Christ as the basis for assembling of all whom He receives as sons into one complete spiritual reality. This reality is called the Body of Christ, and it is the place that contains one's sonship along with the relevant gifts and calling, the economy to support a life in Christ, the positioning and culture within a family of God, and ultimately a complete return to God's original intent for creating humankind, all of which exists and is possible due to the principle of the resurrection of the dead.

The principle of resurrection is one of the foundations of creation. It is essential to the continuity of life on earth. God spoke this principle into creation, saying, "Let the earth bring forth grass, the herb yielding seed, and the fruit tree yielding fruit after his kind, whose seed is in itself, upon the earth: and it was so."[175]

By creating plants and trees whose seed is within themselves, God began a perpetuating cycle of death, resurrection, and life. The Spirit of God so interwove this principle into creation that humankind does not notice, and largely takes for granted, its effects. Jesus summarized the natural occurrence of resurrection, saying, "[U]nless a kernel of wheat falls to the ground and dies, it remains only a single seed. But if it dies, it produces many seeds."[176] However, this passage also foreshadows Jesus's death and the consequences of His own resurrection, identifying the natural occurrence of resurrection that veils the spiritual reality: that Jesus Christ is the resurrection and the life.[177]

> God created the earth to house physical allegories of heaven's transcendent qualities. "For since the creation of the world God's invisible qualities—his eternal power and divine nature—have been clearly seen, being understood from what has been made, so that people are without excuse." [Rom 1:20.] God often chooses to explain great truths of heaven through references to the plant and animal kingdom. So, a son looks like his father, and plants and animals reproduce according to their own kind. These physical representations act as veiled types and shadows that reflect the actual order of heaven.[178]

The unveiled spiritual reality of the resurrection of the dead is just as essential to life in the Spirit as seeds falling to the ground, dying, and rising again as new plants is necessary to the continuity of life on earth.

The Elementary Doctrine, the resurrection of the dead, has two important principles for life and maturity as a believer: One is that resurrection of the dead reconnects humans to God as their source of origin and purpose; the other is that understanding the spiritual principle of resurrection helps one reconnect to the Spirit of God through the process of being born again as a son of God.[179]

The Principle of the Resurrection

Contained in each seed is the ability to duplicate exactly the plant of its origin. Typically, a seed comprises an outer protective casing and an inner core that contains the life to be released. When the seed is buried in the earth, the conditions of its environment, such as moisture and heat, cause a break in the outer casing and activate the life within. This is resurrection: It is the process in which life escapes through the breach in the outer casing and ascends toward the surface to begin its cycle of growth above the place where it was buried. When fully grown and bearing fruit, the plant becomes an exact replica of the one that produced the seed.

It is impossible to ignore the prevalence of this principle in the natural world. Every human being experiences this process on a daily basis. It has been the source of food for humans and animals every day since creation. Yet, many routinely deny the possibility of life coming out of death.

God has used the production of food, being basic to the survival of the human species, to show the eternal principle of the resurrection, which is central to His purposes for placing mankind upon the earth.

God created a perpetual supply of food for as long as He planned that it should take to accomplish these purposes. From this design, one may infer that God planned that many generations should come from Adam. Thus, their existence upon the earth was not merely for the purpose of occupying space or marking time until the end of the age, but for the fulfilling of eternal purposes from one generation to another. So, God said, "As long as the earth endures, *seedtime and harvest*, cold and heat, summer and winter, day and night will never cease" (emphasis added).[180]

Accordingly, the natural occurring resurrection is connected to Jesus's own divine purpose for being in the earth and mankind's destiny as sons of God. "I am the resurrection and the life. He who believes in Me will live, even though he dies; and whoever lives and believes in Me will never die."[181] God always intended that in Christ, resurrection and life would be inseparable components for the life of the believer.

The Seed of the Spirit

The "personhood" of all human beings is their spirit, contained in an outer casing of dust, and every spirit is as a seed issued from the person of God.

God formed Adam's body out of dust and placed a spirit that originated out of God's own person into him. The mind of the human spirit perceives all things from a heavenly point of view. God also gave Adam a soul so that mankind could execute heavenly realities in the venue of time and space. Humans, therefore, have the capacity to represent the invisible God in the visible realm in the manner that a seed replicates the source of its origin.

In personhood and in purpose, "Adam [was] the son of God."[182] Adam's purpose as the seed of the Spirit of God was to display God's nature. The manner of this display was his representation as the son of God. He could put on display both the nature and character of God, his Father, in the domain of earth, over which God placed Adam as the ruler. As a being derived from the personhood of God, Adam was to make the invisible God visible, through representation.

Comprising a body, soul, and spirit, the natural order of Adam's being was that of his spirit being preeminent over his soul, bound to creation by his body. His disobedience and separation from God changed that order when his soul asserted itself as the dominant part of his being, controlling his thoughts and actions:

> When the eyes of the soul were opened, man's view of himself and his purpose in creation underwent a complete change. He transitioned from being a son to becoming fatherless; and in that transition he lost the vision of himself as being spirit, like his Father, and saw himself as flesh.[183]

When the "eyes" of mankind's souls were opened, earthly "wisdom" replaced the heavenly perspective of the human spirit's mind. Immediately, Adam began to see himself only as flesh, rather than spirit merely clothed in flesh, believing that the outer casing is his true being.

This changed perspective altered both his view of reality and his purpose for being in the world. Previously, Adam's purpose was defined by the truth that he was a spirit being designed to replicate God's nature and character, making God visible in the domain of earth. Believing that he was merely flesh changed his imperatives for being, and survival became the primary motivation of his existence.

Adam lived for nearly 1,000 years after the fall, and his views became the foundation for human culture. This culture continued unchanged along that arc until the coming of Christ. Christ came to restore the original order of God's priorities.

Jesus restored the knowledge that God placed His Son in the earth for the benefit of all mankind. This knowledge was lost to the millennia that followed Adam's fall. It had been replaced by types and shadows of the truth, until Jesus Christ was revealed as the Son of God.

> God entered into a covenant with Himself, with the Father and the Son as the parties to the covenant—"since there was no one greater for him to swear by, he swore by himself." The Son's part was to take on human form and to come to earth to be the sacrificial Lamb.[184]

His death and resurrection made it possible for all mankind to be the sons of God.

> The Father's part in the covenant was to accept the sacrifice of the Son as a sufficient atonement for all of the sins of all humankind.[185]

His representation of God on the earth provided an alternative to Adam's departure from his original purpose.

> God would appoint the Son as the mediator of this covenant, thereby giving Him the authority to determine

who would benefit from it. The Father and the Son, working in the perfect harmony defined by this covenantal agreement, would neutralize the effects of Adam's actions, and nullify all of Satan's activities, which are designed to keep man from his destiny as sons and heirs of God. The precreation covenant would reopen the way to God for man, and man could once again view God as his Father and himself as a viceroy of the Kingdom of Heaven.[186]

In Christ Jesus, mankind could be restored to the original intent of God for the creation of man.

Christ's bodily resurrection is the cornerstone of the faith of those who trust in God.

> *But if it is preached that Christ has been raised from the dead, how can some of you say that there is no resurrection of the dead? If there is no resurrection of the dead, then not even Christ has been raised. And if Christ has not been raised, our preaching is useless and so is your faith. More than that, we are then found to be false witnesses about God, for we have testified about God that He raised Christ from the dead. But He did not raise Him if in fact the dead are not raised. For if the dead are not raised, then Christ has not been raised either. And if Christ has not been raised, your faith is futile; you are still in your sins. Then those also who have fallen asleep in Christ are lost* (1 Corinthians 15:12-18 NIV).

The spiritual principle of the resurrection's applicable scope is much greater than the natural principle, which is the daily food supply that supports life on the earth. Resurrection of the dead is the precise manner in which mankind is reconciled to God.

The Resurrection of the Dead

Every human spirit originated from God and was imparted as an endowment from God into what John Milton described as "darksome House of mortal Clay."[187] Every spirit is designed to display some aspect of God's nature in the earth. This is the predestined purpose underlying the creation of every individual.

However, the complete showing of the nature of God is not possible in a single individual. God intended that the complete display of His nature and character be housed in a corporate entity comprising numerous individual parts: "All these are the work of one and the same Spirit, and He distributes them to each one, just as He determines. Just as a body, though one, has many parts, but all its many parts form one body, so it is with Christ."[188] Though the analogy is to the human body, the corporate entity that is referred to is a spiritual body, called the Body of Christ.

The Spirit housed within the body of the man Jesus is the Spirit known as the Christ. Its unique distinction from all other spirits is its ability to receive and assemble all the individual human spirits who are reconciled to God into one corporate form. Each spirit reconciled to God in this manner is regarded appropriately as a son of God, and as an assembled corporate entity, they are together referred to as the Son of God, or alternatively, the Body of Christ. The Lord Jesus Christ is the Head of the Body.[189]

During His brief lifetime, the man Jesus remained connected to God as the obedient Son. The Spirit within Him completely obeyed every instruction from God, even the instruction that resulted in His death on the cross. His perfectly obedient life was the pattern to which all who were to be included in this corporate form would be conformed.

His life on earth is proof that He was the carrier of the corporate Spirit: "Men of Israel, listen to this: Jesus of Nazareth was a man accredited by God to you by miracles, wonders and signs, which God did among you through Him, as you yourselves know."[190] However, as long as He was alive in the flesh, the Spirit within Him remained veiled. His death was necessary in part to release the Spirit of Christ enclosed in His earthly form: "God raised Him from the dead, freeing Him from the agony of death, because it was impossible for death to keep its hold on Him. ... God has raised this Jesus to life, and we are all witnesses of the fact. ... God has made this Jesus, whom you crucified, both Lord and Christ."[191]

No one could be assembled to Him in His earthly form; His resurrection removed the limitations of the human flesh upon His Spirit's existence. He lived and died as a natural man, but was raised as a spiritual man.[192] Because the lesser order is included in the greater order, when He was resurrected as a spiritual man, no part of Him was left in the grave.

Christ's resurrection is as central to life in the Spirit as the sustenance produced by natural resurrection is necessary to natural life on the earth. "If Christ has not been raised, your faith is futile; you are still in your sins. Then those also who have fallen asleep in Christ are lost. If only for this life we have hope in Christ, we are to be pitied more than all men."[193] However, Peter boldly proclaims the resurrection and the life that is in Christ:

> *But Christ has indeed been raised from the dead, the firstfruits of those who have fallen asleep. For since death came through a man, the resurrection of the dead comes also through a man. For as in Adam all die, so in Christ all will be made alive. But each in his own turn: Christ, the firstfruits; then, when He comes, those who belong to Him* (1 Corinthians 15:20-23 NIV).

The Lord Jesus Christ's resurrection released the life within Him, the Spirit known as Christ, for the purpose of reconciling human spirits to God as sons assembled into the corporate whole.

It is in the corporate Son that the identity of man as sons of God is restored. Jesus said, "I am the resurrection and the life. He who believes in Me will live, even though he dies; and whoever lives by believing in Me will never die...."[194] It is only through Christ that mankind is reconciled to God, as His sons.

> *For through Him we both have access to the Father by one Spirit. Consequently, you are no longer foreigners and aliens, but fellow citizens with God's people and members of God's household, built on the foundation of the apostles and prophets, with Christ Jesus Himself as the chief cornerstone. In Him the whole building is joined together and rises to become a holy temple in the Lord. And in Him you too are being built together to become a dwelling in which God lives by His Spirit* (Ephesians 2:18-22 NIV).

Apart from inclusion in the Corpus Christi, there is no access to God and no basis upon which one may refer to God as Father.[195]

In the corporate Christ, one who has been born again of the Spirit is assembled as a part of the Body of Christ. He inherits the glory that God gave to Jesus. This is the glory of calling God "Father," making the one who inherits that glory a son of God.

It was by that glory that Jesus was permitted to enter into a relationship with God as the Son of God. He modeled obedience to the Father and put on display the original intent of God for having a Son. God as Father showed the full scope of His love for humankind through the acts and actions He undertook in and through the person of His obedient Son. The Son chose to do nothing of Himself and limited all of His doings to that which the Father was doing.

Jesus's obedience was in yielding His entire person completely to the dictates of His Father, making Him vulnerable in the extreme. His provision and protection had to be arranged by His Father and delivered moment-by-moment, guaranteed through His Father's love.

Similarly, every word or thought He expressed came from the Father, and every action He undertook was the manner in which His Father chose to express His nature in that moment. These acts revealed the nature of the Father and also revealed Jesus as the Son of the Father.

Before He was known as the Son of God, Christ was known formally as the Word of God:

> *In the beginning was the Word, and the Word was with God, and the Word was God. He was with God in the beginning. Through Him all things were made; without Him nothing was made that has been made. In Him was life, and that life was the light of men. The light shines in the darkness, but the darkness has not understood it* (John 1:1-5 NIV).

Upon His advent into the earth, the Son put aside the power and authority associated with His glory as the Word of God and learned the obedience of a son. Upon the conclusion of His earthly assignment, He took up, once again, the glory of the Word.[196]

The glory of the Word is distinguished from the glory He had on the earth, which was the glory to call God "Father." Upon the completion of His destiny, Jesus returned to the Father to resume the glory He had as the Word.

However, He left the glory He was given while He was in the earth, by sending the Spirit of Sonship back to the earth upon His return to the Father. This is evident from the manner in which He described the manifestation of God that would replace Him in the earth. Concerning the Holy Spirit to come, Christ Jesus said,

> *He will not speak on His own; He will speak only what He hears, and He will tell you what is yet to come. He will bring glory to Me by taking from what is Mine and making it known to you. All that belongs to the Father is Mine. That is why I said the Spirit will take from what is Mine and make it known to you* (John 16:13b-15).

The aspect of the Spirit of God that empowers the corporate Christ continues the work that was begun in the individual Son through the corporate Son. The work of God that was put on display in the man Jesus, can achieve its complete expression in the corporate Son, because the Body of Christ has been given the same glory that

God gave to Jesus. It is the foundation of the inheritance of all those assembled to the Body of Christ, because whoever is assembled to Christ has inherited the right to call God "Father." This is why no one may come to the Father apart from being assembled into the corporate spiritual man.[197] This does not result from any manner of work. Instead, it is the foundation of "the inheritance of the saints in the kingdom of light."[198]

In order to access this glory, one must be born again. The initial birth is that of spirit contained in flesh. The subsequent birth is that spirit, beginning the process by which spirit becomes preeminent over flesh.

Concerning these two births, Jesus said, "Flesh gives birth to flesh, but the Spirit gives birth to spirit. You should not be surprised at My saying, 'You must be born again.'"[199] The process of this new birth is that of spirit, being released from its control by the flesh, through the process of death and resurrection.[200]

The Elementary Doctrine of the resurrection of the dead is in part designed to acquaint the believer with the certainty of change. After the initial spiritual birth, one begins the stage of growing up into a mature son of God, leading ultimately to a mature or exact representation of Christ.

Paul speaks to his own growth in this regard by writing, "When I was a child, I talked like a child, I thought like a child, I reasoned like a child. When I became a man, I put childish ways behind me."[201]

Each of the stages of maturity involves the process of dying to the old and being resurrected to the new. One ascends from glory to glory, the latter being the place of accurate representation of the Father.

The process of resurrection is engaged initially when one is born again and subsequently throughout all the stages of growth and maturity. So, it can be said that one "dies daily" and is resurrected daily. One should, therefore, not be embarrassed that God requires change as a constant part of the process of maturing. This change is so complete that it can be compared only to the metamorphosis inherent in the process of death and resurrection.

I am the Resurrection and the Life

> *"Lord," Martha said to Jesus, "if You had been here, my brother would not have died. But I know that even now God will give You whatever You ask." Jesus said to her, "Your brother will rise again." Martha answered, "I know he will rise again in the resurrection at the last day." Jesus said to her, "I am the resurrection and the life. He who believes in Me will live, even though he dies; and whoever lives and believes in Me will never die. Do you believe this?"* (John 11:21-26 NIV)

In this exchange with Martha, Jesus revealed one of the most astonishing mysteries of who He was on the earth.

In discussing the possibility of resurrection, Martha's response—stating that there is a day of resurrection at which time the dead will be raised physically—represented the common understanding of resurrection. But, Jesus was speaking of Himself; and Lazarus's death and resurrection were designed to reveal the great truth about Christ: that He is "the resurrection and the life."

Every incidence of resurrection that occurs in nature was intended to be understood as a shadow of this superlative reality. As the Spirit of Christ, He resided in the Body of Jesus, waiting for the appointed time in which, through His own death and resurrection, God would establish His spiritual presence on the earth with both the capability and the intent of assembling all those who desired to be reconciled to Him into the Body of Christ.

Life was contained in the outer casing of Jesus's mortal clay. This is life that is indestructible, because it is vested in a spirit being. The source of this life is not derived from the world around it. Instead, its continuity is as a result of having been issued originally from the person of God Himself. This is described as life on earth sustained from the realm of the eternal. It is, therefore, eternal life.

The Resurrection of the Dead

The Spirit of Christ was a seed contained within a body. The seed had to undergo the process of death and resurrection to display fully God's glory, which the Son came to reveal in the earth. He was the resurrection and the life, because God had come in the humility of human flesh to be killed, buried, and on the third day to be raised again to life, and in that process was the salvation of all mankind. To emphasize this declaration, Jesus raised Lazarus from the dead, in a demonstration of the power of God.

Now, whoever has been assembled to Christ becomes a partaker of the life that is within the person of Christ.

When Jesus was raised from the dead, the form of His resurrection was new and unique. He was put into the grave as a natural man, but the body that came forth was a spiritual body. The natural body did not remain in the ground, but arose as the spiritual being that was always housed in the natural.

There is no death in the Spirit:

> *For we know that since Christ was raised from the dead, He cannot die again; death no longer has mastery over Him. The death He died, He died to sin once for all; but the life He lives, He lives to God. In the same way, count yourselves dead to sin but alive to God in Christ Jesus* (Romans 6:9-11 NIV).

Natural bodies will be subject to death; it is to be understood that all natural aspects of the human being will eventually return to the dust. Death, however, is to be understood as a permanent separation of the human spirit from the source of its origin, and until one is reconciled to God, he lives in a state of death although he has a spirit, because he has been disconnected from the source that maintains the life of his spirit.

Jesus was put on the earth as the point of contact between the spirits of mankind and the Spirit of God. The Spirit of Christ, contained within the man Jesus, carried the life of God. It was from this source that the life of God could be imparted to man. Therefore, whomever God receives as a son, He assembles into the Body of Christ. In this manner, one who has been previously separated from God is reconnected to the source of his life. He, therefore, can never die and passes from death to life.[202]

On the occasion of the resurrection of Lazarus from the dead, Jesus first declared He is the resurrection and the life. He established this declaration through the act of calling Lazarus back from the dead. In response, an already decaying corpse that had been placed in the tomb four days earlier stirred to life and came forth. Lazarus was resurrected from the dead. By His declaration and His action, Jesus demonstrated the truth of the resurrection and revealed that He is the source of resurrection and life.

Questions Relating to the Resurrection of the Dead

There are many theories and much confusion surrounding the question of resurrection in the Scriptures. Most of these questions result from a general overemphasis on going to Heaven among religious groups. Various theories have taken root that surround the resurrection of the dead, but in cleaving to a theology based upon going to Heaven, they ignore certain key concepts. The focus tends to turn to eschatological or end-times theories. Though these issues are not central to the elementary principle of the resurrection of the dead, they are important issues to examine for a more complete understanding of resurrection in Scripture.

> *But someone may ask, "How are the dead raised? With what kind of body will they come?" How foolish! What you sow does not come to life unless it dies. When you sow, you do not plant the body that will be, but just a seed, perhaps of wheat or of something else. But God gives it a body as He has determined, and to each kind of seed He gives its own body. All flesh is not the same: Men have one kind of flesh, animals have another, birds another*

and fish another. There are also heavenly bodies and there are earthly bodies; but the splendor of the heavenly bodies is one kind, and the splendor of the earthly bodies is another. The sun has one kind of splendor, the moon another and the stars another; and star differs from star in splendor. So will it be with the resurrection of the dead. The body that is sown is perishable, it is raised imperishable; it is sown in dishonor, it is raised in glory; it is sown in weakness, it is raised in power; it is sown a natural body, it is raised a spiritual body. If there is a natural body, there is also a spiritual body. So it is written: "The first man Adam became a living being"; the last Adam, a life-giving spirit. The spiritual did not come first, but the natural, and after that the spiritual. The first man was of the dust of the earth, the second man from heaven. As was the earthly man, so are those who are of the earth; and as is the man from heaven, so also are those who are of heaven. And just as we have borne the likeness of the earthly man, so shall we bear the likeness of the man from heaven. I declare to you, brothers, that flesh and blood cannot inherit the kingdom of God, nor does the perishable inherit the imperishable. Listen, I tell you a mystery: We will not all sleep, but we will all be changed—in a flash, in the twinkling of an eye, at the last trumpet. For the trumpet will sound, the dead will be raised imperishable, and we will be changed. For the perishable must clothe itself with the imperishable, and the mortal with immortality. ... "Where, O death, is your victory? Where, O death, is your sting?"
(1 Corinthians 15:35-53,55 NIV)

The First Resurrection and the Rapture

Perhaps the most common end-times theory that surrounds certain elements of resurrection is "the Rapture."

This concept takes various forms. The most common form is the belief that all believers in Christ present on the earth will be suddenly removed from the earth to Heaven at the beginning of the Great Tribulation, where they will wait out this seven-year period.

The idea is that God will remove them from the earth to keep them from suffering as the rest of humanity endures both the rampage of the Beast and God's retribution.

The Rapture theory is predicated upon the scriptural time of the resurrection of the dead, at the end of the age, when Christ returns to the earth.[203] However, it is not clearly understood as the resurrection of the dead, merely as the transformation and rescue of believers in Christ; and it ignores the basic concept and much of the details surrounding the sudden transformation of the living believers in Scripture.

Scripture describes the resurrection of the dead at the end of the age or "the first resurrection," as occurring on the day of the Lord's return from Heaven:

> *We believe that Jesus died and rose again and so we believe that God will bring with Jesus those who have fallen asleep in Him. According to the Lord's own word, we tell you that we who are still alive, who are left until the coming of the Lord, will certainly not precede those who have fallen asleep. For the Lord Himself will come down from heaven, with a loud command, with the voice of the archangel and with the trumpet call of God, and the dead in Christ will rise first. After that, we who are still alive and are left will be caught up together with them in the clouds to meet the Lord in the air. And so we will be with the Lord forever* (1 Thessalonians 4:14-17 NIV).

This event involves both the resurrection of the dead in Christ and, subsequently, the sudden transformation of those still living:

> *Listen, I tell you a mystery: We will not all sleep, but we will all be changed—in a flash, in the twinkling of an eye, at the last trumpet. For the trumpet will sound, the dead will be raised imperishable, and we will be changed. For the perishable must clothe itself with the imperishable, and the mortal with immortality* (1 Corinthians 15:51-53 NIV).

Together they will be caught up to the clouds. Note that no one will be caught up to heaven, only to the clouds.

In further contrast to the Rapture theory, upon being raised and/or changed, they will return with Christ to the earth.

> *They had not worshiped the beast or its image and had not received its mark on their foreheads or their hands. They came to life and reigned with Christ a thousand years. (The rest of the dead did not come to life until the thousand years were ended.) This is the first resurrection* (Revelation 20:4b-5 NIV).

This first resurrection begins a thousand-year reign on the earth with Christ:

> *Blessed and holy are those who have part in the first resurrection. The second death has no power over them, but they will be priests of God and of Christ and will reign with Him for a thousand years* (Revelation 20:6 NIV).

This event definitively concludes the current age.

Jesus gave the disciples a detailed account of "the sign of [His] coming and of the end of the age," which will be the time when those who have died in Christ will be resurrected.[204] Jesus described events and circumstances at the time of His actual, physical return, and later, angels confirmed that Christ would return.[205] There will be no secret to the return of the Lord; it is meant to be the most arresting event in all of human history.

As opposed to the narrow view of the Rapture as an opportunity to escape to Heaven, resurrection itself is a much more significant concept in Scripture. It describes the condition that results when one has become victorious over death.

> *When the perishable has been clothed with the imperishable, and the mortal with immortality, then the saying that is written will come true: "Death has been swallowed up in victory." "Where, O death, is your victory? Where, O death, is your sting?" The sting of death is sin, and the power of sin is the law. But thanks be to God! He gives us the victory through our Lord Jesus Christ* (1 Corinthians 15:54-57 NIV).

Resurrection applies only after one has died, physically or symbolically. Resurrection provides a complete transformation in the nature of the being, one that is free from the consequences of sin and death. Even for those still physically alive, post resurrection existence is sufficiently different from one's former life, so that the person is an entirely new being:

> The only way forward is through resurrection. The person coming through this process begins a new life as a resurrected being and a new creation. There is no truth in any condemnation of sin rooted in the old life, and through the continual process of repentance and the renewing of the mind, the person is freed from the consequences of sin.[206]

The Form in Which the Dead Are Resurrected

"But someone may ask, 'How are the dead raised? With what kind of body will they come?'"[207] Paul proceeds to answer this question fully:

When you sow, you do not plant the body that will be, but just a seed, perhaps of wheat or of something else. But God gives it a body as He has determined, and to each kind of seed He gives its own body. All flesh is not the same: Men have one kind of flesh, animals have another, birds another and fish another. There are also heavenly bodies and there are earthly bodies; but the splendor of the heavenly bodies is one kind, and the splendor of the earthly bodies is another. The sun has one kind of splendor, the moon another and the stars another; and star differs from star in splendor. So will it be with the resurrection of the dead. The body that is sown is perishable, it is raised imperishable; it is sown in dishonor, it is raised in glory; it is sown in weakness, it is raised in power; it is sown a natural body, it is raised a spiritual body. If there is a natural body, there is also a spiritual body. So it is written: "The first man Adam became a living being"; the last Adam, a life-giving spirit. The spiritual did not come first, but the natural, and after that the spiritual. The first man was of the dust of the earth; the second man from heaven. As was the earthly man, so are those who are of the earth; and as is the man from heaven, so also are those who are of heaven. And just as we have borne the likeness of the earthly man, so shall we bear the likeness of the man from heaven. I declare to you, brothers, that flesh and blood cannot inherit the kingdom of God, nor does the perishable inherit the imperishable. Listen, I tell you a mystery: We will not all sleep, but we will all be changed—in a flash, in the twinkling of an eye, at the last trumpet. For the trumpet will sound, the dead will be raised imperishable, and we will be changed. For the perishable must clothe itself with the imperishable, and the mortal with immortality. When the perishable has been clothed with the imperishable, and the mortal with immortality, then the saying that is written will come true: "Death has been swallowed up in victory." "Where, O death, is your victory? Where, O death, is your sting?" The sting of death is sin, and the power of sin is the law. But thanks be to God! He gives us the victory through our Lord Jesus Christ. Therefore, my dear brothers, stand firm. Let nothing move you. Always give yourselves fully to the work of the Lord, because you know that your labor in the Lord is not in vain (1 Corinthians 15:37-58 NIV).

He first explained that when you sow, you are not planting the results that will come, but the seed from which the results will come. So then, if one plants an acorn, an oak tree will come up out of the acorn, an order exponentially greater than the thing that was planted. He offers as an explanation the fact that this phenomenon is readily visible in nature, noting that there are many different kinds of bodies on the earth, such as birds, fish, and animals.

He extends the comparison to the heavens and compares heavenly bodies and their splendors with the earth. The earth is different from the sun, the moon, and the stars; and even the stars are different from one another in both their environments and their splendors. He uses this analogy to compare the natural body to the spiritual, and in that comparison, he observes that the natural body is perishable, weak, and degenerates over time.

Whereas the spiritual body is imperishable, glorious, and powerful, Paul firmly asserts that, as surely as there is a natural body, there is also a spiritual body that comes after the natural. He concludes that "just as we have borne the image of the earthly man, so shall we bear the image of the heavenly man," referring to Adam and Jesus Christ, respectively.

The resurrection will supply a spiritual body in the place of the natural.

We will not all sleep, but we will all be changed—in a flash, in the twinkling of an eye, at the last trumpet. For the trumpet will sound, the dead will be raised imperishable, and we will be changed. For the perishable must clothe itself with the imperishable, and the mortal with immortality. When the perishable has been clothed with the imperishable, and the mortal with immortality, then the saying that is written will come true: "Death has been swallowed up in victory" (1 Corinthians 15:51b-54 NIV).

Jesus is "the firstfruits" of those who died: He was crucified in His natural body and died; and He was raised in His spiritual body as the Christ. He did not leave behind, in the grave, a remnant of His previous, natural form; the lesser form is included in the greater, spiritual form.

Body, Soul, and Spirit

One of the related questions to the resurrection is whether resurrection serves any purpose for those who are taken to Heaven when they die. To understand the need for the resurrection after a person has died, it is necessary to have a more complete picture of what God intended.

God gave human beings spirits to connect mankind to God. Through the spirit, every person has access to the heavenly realms and understanding regarding God's intent for the creation of the world. God also gave the human a soul so that each person could translate the understanding of the heavens and of God into a practical and functional administration in the world. God encased both spirit and soul in a physical body, anchoring them in the venue of earth. These three distinct elements—spirit, soul, and body—are each fated for a different destination after the body dies.

At the point of physical death, these three components separate.

Then man goes to his eternal home and mourners go about the streets. Remember him—before the silver cord is severed, or the golden bowl is broken; before the pitcher is shattered at the spring, or the wheel broken at the well, and the dust returns to the ground it came from, and the spirit returns to God who gave it (Ecclesiastes 12:5-7 NIV).

When the body dies, the container of the spirit and the soul is lost, and one relinquishes the connection to the natural world. The human spirit returns to God, the origin from which it came. And, depending upon whether the person had been assembled to the Body of Christ or not, the soul goes to Heaven or to hell.[208]

The body is confined to the dust of the earth, from which it was originally made. It must be noted that it is the only one of the three elements of one's being that actually dies. Therefore, it is the only element of man subject to resurrection. The spirit remains alive and so does the soul, but they are no longer tied to the natural world.[209]

The Second Resurrection and the Final Judgment

Bodily resurrection will occur for those who died in Christ at the time of the first resurrection and the return of Christ. For the unbeliever, however, there is a second resurrection. This resurrection of the unrighteous dead will occur at the end of the millennium that follows Christ's return:

> *(The rest of the dead did not come to life until the thousand years were ended.) ... Then I saw a great white throne and Him who was seated on it. Earth and sky fled from His presence, and there was no place for them. And I saw the dead, great and small, standing before the throne, and books were opened. Another book was opened, which is the book of life. The dead were judged according to what they had done as recorded in the books. The sea gave up the dead that were in it, and death and Hades gave up the dead that were in them, and each person was judged according to what he had done. Then death and Hades were thrown into the lake of fire. The lake of fire is the second death. If anyone's name was not found written in the book*

of life, he was thrown into the lake of fire (Revelation 20:5,11-15 NIV).

At that time, those who were not part of the first resurrection will be raised to face the judgment of God as they stand before the great white throne at the end of the millennium.

Whoever is born again of the Spirit is assembled into this body and has the legitimate right to call God his Father. Indeed, the first cry of every newborn believer is the cry of recognition of God as his Father: "Father! Father!"[210]

In the person of Christ, one is restored to the original plan of God for his or her life upon the earth and empowered by the economy designed to support the spiritual man. Such a person is a new creation, born of Spirit, assembled to Christ, and received by God as a son. This is a truth of which none of the enemy's deceptions can prevail. It establishes the believer as a spiritual being who cannot be separated from the love of God.

CHAPTER SIX
ETERNAL JUDGMENT

The doctrine of *Eternal Judgment* appropriately comes at the end of the study on the Elementary Doctrines.

Internally, within the Body of Christ, administration of this doctrine is judgment amongst believers. This is an administration reserved primarily for mature sons of God, but its necessity is one that secures the order of the House of God.

Externally, it is the order of the Body of Christ, secured and displayed through eternal judgment, that presents a righteous standard in creation by which God may judge all things.

Through eternal judgment, the standards of the Kingdom of Heaven are brought to the earth for the purpose of showing the alternative to the limited, bias, and prejudicial standards of the nations of mankind. Perhaps more than any other feature of life in the Kingdom of God, eternal judgment distinguishes and ennobles the people of God among the peoples of the earth.

It is impossible to judge any matter apart from the existence of a standard. Because the standards of righteousness have long been absent from both the world and the church, the accurate portrayal of the nature of God ha declined dramatically in the modern world. The restoration of both the doctrine and practice of eternal judgment to the Body of Christ is a prophetic signal that God means to cause judgment to come, first to the House of God.

Once the Body of Christ has been accurately realigned to the righteousness of God, then God will inevitably use this perfected standard to bring the world to judgment. It must be noted that God's intent in applying the standards of righteousness to mankind is to correct the deviation from his original nature and to bring about reconciliation. This process determines what may be saved and what is without use and must be discarded.

Judge Not Lest You Be Judged

The Scripture most often cited as a prohibition against judging others is actually a warning against the judgment of unqualified judges and the use of unrighteous standards:

> *Do not judge, or you too will be judged. For in the same way you judge others, you will be judged, and with the measure you use, it will be measured to you. Why do you look at the speck of sawdust in your brother's eye and pay no attention to the plank in your own eye? How can you say to your brother, "Let me take the speck out of your eye," when all the time there is a plank in your own eye? You hypocrite, first take the plank out of your own eye, and then you will see clearly to remove the speck from your brother's eye* (Matthew 7:1-5 NIV).

This passage warns a person, who is presuming to pass judgment, against using unrighteous standards. Among other problems exists the likelihood that the one judging will be judged by the same prejudicial standard.

The unqualified judge is a person who lacks the clarity to judge, yet insists on judging others while willfully (or unknowingly) disregarding the failings that cloud one's judgment. A prejudicial judge who lacks clarity cannot employ an eternal standard.

The admonition is to fix those faults that lead one to apply prejudicial standards as a prerequisite to making righteous judgments. It is

Eternal Judgment

not a blanket prohibition against judging or even the eventual judging of the specific matter. Before one can judge a matter, that person must have been subject to the removal of conditions that would lead inevitably to a distortion of judgment. If the judge is not so qualified, then the process of eternal judgment is flawed from the beginning and cannot result in righteousness and peace.

Contrary to the popular belief that the Bible instructs not to judge one another, Scripture makes clear that judging within the Body of Christ is necessary to its proper functioning:

> *What business is it of mine to judge those outside the church? Are you not to judge those inside? God will judge those outside. "Expel the wicked man from among you"* (1 Corinthians 5:12-13 NIV).

Paul warned the New Testament Church against submitting internal disputes to the secular authorities:

> *If any of you has a dispute with another, dare he take it before the ungodly for judgment instead of before the saints? Do you not know that the saints will judge the world? And if you are to judge the world, are you not competent to judge trivial cases? Do you not know that we will judge angels? How much more the things of this life! Therefore, if you have disputes about such matters, appoint as judges even men of little account in the church! I say this to shame you* (1 Corinthians 6:1-5a NIV).

He also made clear that disputes would arise, but that the believers themselves needed to settle these disputes:

> *Is it possible that there is nobody among you wise enough to judge a dispute between believers? But instead, one brother goes to law against another—and this in front of unbeliev-*

ers! The very fact that you have lawsuits among you means you have been completely defeated already. Why not rather be wronged? Why not rather be cheated? (1 Corinthians 6:5-7 NIV)

Invariably, disputes will arise among the people of God, threatening to disrupt the good order that the Holy Spirit seeks for the Body of Christ. All manner of things must be settled in order for believers to live at peace with one another, but it is clear that believers should not submit these matters to the judgments of secular authorities.

While it is wrong for a believer to judge matters if he or she is unqualified, dealing with conflict internally is still necessary for the Body of Christ to function in proper order.

The Elementary Doctrine of Eternal Judgment is the foundation for righteous judgment among believers, and it is the necessary principle for establishing (or reestablishing) divine order in the Body.

Eternal Judgment can be thought of in four basic concepts: (1) the qualified judge; (2) the eternal standard; (3) application of the standard; and (4) determining the outcome or verdict. This process is necessary for the maturing of the Body, and it is a critical role for the mature believer.

The Qualified Judge

If no one is qualified to judge, then the standards of righteousness become clouded as critically important matters go untended. Absent the administration of righteous standards, all manner of evil can infiltrate the ranks of the people of God. The young are devastated by such lack of clarity, and an environment in which no one is held accountable discourages the older and more mature believers. Without qualified judges available to apply eternal standards, the standards of righteousness are reduced to indistinct and incoherent forms. If eternal standards are not employed, then the people are unable to distinguish the false standards from the true and are, therefore, unable to determine what is godly and what is worldly.

The qualified judge removes false and inappropriate standards and restores divine order. The absence of a righteous standard, however, is the classic biblical definition of lawlessness—everyone doing what is right in their own eyes.[211] Lawlessness and false standards lead to chaos, disorder, and the disruption of the Body of Christ.[212] Whereas, eternal judgment is the accurate application of eternal standards to human conflict, and this Elementary Doctrine brings order when chaos would otherwise dominate the people.

Eternal judgment redeems conflict, which would be wholly divisive in the secular world. Among believers, however, conflict can yield the most valuable results—uncovering the areas in which growth toward maturity is most needed and restoring lost relationships.

Until conflict arises, one's hidden impediments to maturity may remain firmly in place, influencing both thought and behavior. Conflict disturbs settled conditions and brings things hidden away in the deep places of a person's soul to the surface. The accurate handling of disputes often permits the best chance for growth possible among believers. However, it is imperative that the process of judging strictly observe divine protocol.

A Divine Standard of Judgment

The first element of the divine protocol for righteous judgment is the standard that the qualified judge will apply—called an eternal, divine, or righteous standard. God's intent in eternal judgment is for His nature and character to be the measuring stick of human behavior.[213] This is an eternal and, therefore, a necessarily unbiased, non-prejudicial standard. Whereas a prejudicial standard is rooted in the human failings of an individual,[214] a divine or eternal standard represents the importation of the character of God as the measuring stick of human behavior.

The standard is God. Those whom the Holy Spirit has assembled into Christ, the Son, are His earthly representations:

> *In the past God spoke to our forefathers through the prophets at many times and in various ways, but in these last*

> *days He has spoken to us by His Son, whom He appointed heir of all things, and through whom He made the universe. The Son is the radiance of God's glory and the exact representation of His being, sustaining all things by His powerful word* (Hebrews 1:1-3a NIV).

Any judgment rendered within the Body of Christ must be consistent with how God would judge the matter. Moreover, the mature son of God is the instrument through which God Himself judges the matter.

Regarding the resolution of conflicts and judgments rendered therein, Jesus taught that "whatever you bind on earth will be bound in heaven, and whatever you loose on earth will be loosed in heaven."[215] An eternal standard of judgment requires mankind to adopt both God's standards and His character in the substance and form of judgments rendered. In doing so, eternal judgment is rendered by God's representatives, on His behalf, but this requirement also makes the administration of the eternal standard the prerogative of mature sons.

The substance of an eternal standard is one of perspective. An eternal standard views human events from a position of timelessness. A temporal standard is limited by time and the resulting urgencies determined by mankind's imperatives. An eternal standard is unmotivated by human priorities. It is a standard that runs true to eternal values, but furthers them in a temporal context. Eternal standards are consistent with the unfolding of God's plans within human circumstances viewed from a heavenly perspective.

Moreover, an eternal standard may bring to bear certain aspects of God's nature to prevent great loss to the Household of Faith. God's nature includes qualities such as mercy, grace, and forgiveness; whereas rigidly biased human standards of judgment have no place for such qualities, even though these qualities might preserve and ultimately redeem the one being judged. The intent of all spiritual judgments is to redeem and restore the one being judged to his or her eternal destiny to the maximum extent possible.

Examples of the power of an eternal standard abound in Scripture. If the young Saul of Tarsus (the apostle Paul) had been judged solely upon his actions, human standards of justice and retribution would require the forfeiture of his life. He had persecuted Christ's followers, harassed and imprisoned many early believers, and arranged Stephen's murder.[216] Yet God judged Paul by an eternal standard that included God's plan for Paul's life. Instructing Ananias, a disciple in the city of Damascus, to go and visit Paul, God revealed His plan for Paul's life:

> *"Lord," Ananias answered, "I have heard many reports about this man and all the harm he has done to Your saints in Jerusalem. And he has come here with authority from the chief priests to arrest all who call on Your name." But the Lord said to Ananias, "Go! This man is My chosen instrument to carry My name before the Gentiles and their kings and before the people of Israel. I will show him how much he must suffer for My name"* (Acts 9:13-16 NIV).

If judged by human standards, Paul would have been lost to the House of God before he could be redeemed to become one of the leading figures of the early Church.

Peter was similarly redeemed by an eternal standard. During Christ's arrest and trial, Peter swore vehemently that he did not know Jesus; faced with the possibility of being arrested and tried alongside Jesus, he disavowed any knowledge of the Messiah.[217]

But, Jesus was undeterred by Peter's denial. Later, when Jesus was commissioning Peter, saying "feed My sheep," Christ looked beyond the moments of Peter's weakness to the certainty of his calling.[218] God revealed to Jesus that He had chosen Peter to present the truth of Christ, first to the Jewish people and then to the Gentiles.[219]

An eternal standard originates from the viewpoint of the throne of God and permits the introduction of characteristics of God that are inaccessible to human standards of judgment. Judging from an eternal point of view, one sees what God knows about a person, situation, or the future and then can judge the matter in a manner consistent with God's unfolding purposes.

> *The Lord said to Samuel, "Do not consider his appearance or his height, for I have rejected him. The Lord does not look at the things man looks at. Man looks at the outward appearance, but the Lord looks at the heart"* (1 Samuel 16:7 NIV).

Normal human judgments are limited to the way things appear and the facts surrounding the events that have transpired.

> *For the word of God is living and active. Sharper than any double-edged sword, it penetrates even to dividing soul and spirit, joints and marrow; it judges the thoughts and attitudes of the heart. Nothing in all creation is hidden from God's sight. Everything is uncovered and laid bare before the eyes of Him to whom we must give account* (Hebrews 4:12-13 NIV).

But, God judges the heart.

Judgment from an eternal point of view brings the Kingdom of God more completely into the earth. By contrast, unrighteous judgment discards eternal value as unimportant, because it is incapable of understanding or appreciating the value of the eternal.

Jesus cautioned His disciples about submitting things that may have great eternal value to unrighteous judgment, which has no concept of the eternal: "Do not give dogs what is sacred; do not throw your pearls to pigs. If you do, they may trample them under their feet, and then turn and tear you to pieces."[220] Judgment cannot be placed in the hands of one unequipped to apply an eternal standard, because that judge is likely to discard persons and things of great eternal value through temporal and linear judgments.

Applying the Eternal Standard

There is a precise format for the application of righteous judgment. It begins with determining the authority to judge the matter. Regarding the standards of eternal judgment, Scripture cautions the believer not to judge the unbeliever by divine standards.

> *For God did not send His Son into the world to condemn the world, but to save the world through Him. Whoever believes in Him is not condemned, but whoever does not believe stands condemned already because he has not believed in the name of God's one and only Son. This is the verdict: Light has come into the world, but men loved darkness instead of light because their deeds were evil. Everyone who does evil hates the light, and will not come into the light for fear that his deeds will be exposed. But whoever lives by the truth comes into the light, so that it may be seen plainly that what he has done has been done through God* (John 3:17-21 NIV).

This limits the sphere of judgment over which the believer may exercise divine authority to the House of God. Even when the believer is invited to judge matters among unbelievers, that person should refrain from applying divine standards, since the jurisdiction of the righteous does not extend to include the unrighteous.[221] The unrighteous are condemned already, and therefore, judgment that establishes guilt rather than redemption is superfluous.

A believer who is placed in the position of judging outside of the House of God is not at liberty to employ divine standards as the basis of judgment. Instead, he or she is limited to the applicable rules established by the governing authority.

For example, a believer who is part of the judicial system must judge matters on the basis of the appropriate secular laws and is barred from introducing divine standards such as mercy, forgiveness, and reconciliation as part of the available remedies, though such standards permeate the resolution of disputes among believers.

Therefore, the first step in the process of applying an eternal standard is the accurate determination of who has the authority to judge in the matter at hand. Even among believers, the one who is required to judge must have a sufficient relationship to the person or circumstance subject to judgment. Generally, matters concerning the entire House of God require apostles as judges, though apostles may also judge personal matters, typically those that have far-reaching effects.[222] The matter itself often gives rise to the appropriate judge.

The next procedural step is to accurately determine the true facts. This step is critical and must be undertaken without bias or prejudice. Divine judgment cannot be issued if the underlying facts are inaccurate. It may become necessary to corroborate the facts. If the circumstances require corroboration but is difficult to obtain, it may be appropriate to suspend the process until the facts become clear and incontrovertible. If what is alleged is true, but the judge is unable to corroborate the facts at the time of the allegation, then it is certain that the behavior will reoccur, and at that time, judgment may proceed.[223] This step may require the patience of a mature son to let the matter ripen so that the judge may properly employ the righteousness of the appropriate eternal standard.

The next step is to bring forth the appropriate standard by which to assess the facts. This too is a critical step that may be subject to prejudice and the taint of evil. If the appropriate standard is not employed, the results will be disastrous.

Jesus demonstrated the manner and form of an eternal standard when He was tempted in the wilderness. Satan first tempted Jesus by trying to convince Him to turn stones into bread.[224]

Jesus had just concluded forty days of fasting, and He was very hungry. Satan's temptation was meant to exploit His weakened condition and His gnawing hunger. Subsequently, Jesus judged the enemy's words by bringing out the accurate standard, saying, "It is written: 'Man does not live on bread alone, but on every word that comes from the mouth of God.'"[225] In bringing out this standard, Jesus returned the focus to the spirit over the soul and did not depart from His position as the approved Son of the Father.

Being quick to learn how Jesus judged matters, the enemy thought to confuse the issue by appearing to bring out his own version of an eternal standard with the next temptation.

As Jesus was taken to the pinnacle of the temple, the enemy invited Jesus to throw Himself down from the highest point of the temple, with the admonition, "It is written: 'He will command His angels concerning You, and they will lift You up in their hands, so that You will not strike Your foot against a stone.'"[226]

Jesus corrected Satan by bringing out the appropriate standard: "Jesus answered him, 'It is also written: "Do not put the Lord your God to the test."'"[227]

Although Satan exactly quoted prophetic Scripture regarding Jesus, it was not the appropriate standard.

Jesus would not consent to an inaccurate standard because He knew the mind of the Lord.

It is possible for those who have authority to judge matters to bring an inexact standard. In order to distinguish between the correct standard and an inappropriate one, an absolute symmetry must exist between the letter of Scripture defining the standard and the Spirit of God, which adheres accurately to and discloses God's intent in judging the matter.

It was easy for Jesus to deflect the enemy's attempt to induce Him to employ an incorrect standard. Indeed, the enemy's efforts were transparently manipulative and designed to bring about Jesus's physical death. In the temptation, the intent was not to receive Jesus as the Son of God and to obey Him.

From the beginning, the enemy's *modus operandi* has been to use the Scriptures as a weapon designed for destruction. Satan intended to bring about death and destruction with the accurately quoted Scripture. This contrasts starkly with the purpose of God. In this way, it was patently obvious that the intent behind the proffered standard was inconsistent with God's nature and His intent for Jesus.

Even if the standard for judgment is biblically based and may represent an exact quotation of Scripture, it is necessary to take the next step and to examine the motive and likely outcome behind the standard that is presented. Even if the Scriptures are accurately quoted, the issue becomes the intent of the person offering that standard. If the foreseeable result of the application of that standard is inconsistent with the nature of God, then the standard is not the appropriate one.

However, if there is consistency between the standard and the redemptive nature of God, even if the immediate consequences may be quite drastic, it is likely the right standard.

For example, eternal judgment may require the exclusion of an immoral brother from the fellowship of believers.[228] In the short run, this judgment may appear to be an unloving decision, but as a last resort, it may be the action required to expose the level of deception into which an errant believer may have fallen.

If it is understood that this standard is applied as a last resort to destroy a rebellious believer's resistance to the truth, as contrasted with exclusion from the fellowship, because he has become unsavory, then God is able to bring redemption even through this extreme act.

The Verdict

Once the appropriate standard has been brought forth and applied without prejudice, then the outcome will reflect the will of God. An example of this judgment occurred when God brought judgment to the reign of Belshazzar, the nephew of Nebuchadnezzar. In the midst of feasting, a hand appeared and wrote on the wall of the palace. Daniel translated and interpreted this sign:

> *This is the inscription that was written: mene, mene, tekel, parsin. This is what these words mean: Mene: God has numbered the days of your reign and brought it to an end. Tekel: You have been weighed on the scales and found wanting. Peres: Your kingdom is divided and given to the Medes and Persians* (Daniel 5:25-28 NIV).

Belshazzar's reign had been brought under the scrutiny of God's judgment. The scales are a metaphor for the accuracy of the measurements and templates of God's judgments and the unbiased application of this standard of judgment. God issued a verdict regarding Belshazzar's reign; the scales were unbalanced. The verdict was not in Belshazzar's favor. The final stage of this process is the decree that frames the will of God.

God could have chosen mercy, but since there was no eternal purpose in prolonging Belshazzar's reign, mercy was not the appropriate decree. Belshazzar's kingdom was taken out of his hands and given over to conquerors.[229]

This is one of numerous examples of judgments that occur throughout the Scriptures. Throughout all the examples, the procedures of righteous judgment are clear and distinct. There is a qualified judge, an eternal standard, the application of the standard, and a decree consistent with the will of God for the one being judged. Quite often the purpose of judgment itself and the accompanying decrees are to bring confrontation in order to remove blockages to the purposes of God. Always, the goal of eternal judgment is to restore divine order.

Eternal Judgment and Changing Seasons

The eternal realm is different from the realm of time. Eternal perspectives are advanced in time through incremental changes. In time, these increments are linear, and are understood in terms of past, present, and future; but in the eternal, the end of every matter is known from the beginning. God's unchanging, omniscient nature, which is inclusive of His present knowledge of all things—even things yet to occur in time—is presented as the "Alpha and the Omega…who is and who was and who is to come."[230] God never changes. But, in the way that the unmoving sun appears to move across the daytime sky as the earth rotates, from the linear perspective of the temporal world, God may appear to change.

Time permits the revealing of all the details as well as the processes that underlie the purposes of God. Since God knows the end of every matter and the outcome of every process before they are launched in time, each increment of the unfolding is consistent with what is already known. Things in Heaven are meant to come into the earth and be seen on earth as they are in Heaven in their due and appointed times.

It is impossible to be in harmony with heavenly mandates while seeking certainty by predicting the future as an extension of the past. People's tendency is to attempt to control all the events that affect their lives. This creates the illusion of control that comes through predictability. However, the tendency to retain control of one's circumstances by any means is inherently in conflict with God's intent to host eternal events and show divine processes in time. Eternal things are meant to change the trajectory of unfolding events to eternal purposes, confounding human predictability.

Remaining dedicated to that which seems predictable based on past events, even in the face of true change, will cause one to conflict directly with God's purposes. Religious organizations and institutions that sow human traditions and culture as a form of control over the people shows the nature of this inherent conflict.

Since the Emperor Constantine in the early 4th Century AD made the church the official religion of the Roman Empire, the emphasis of this religious pattern in the ensuing two millennia has been to thoroughly infuse itself into the culture of people groups and to define the people's history though religious practices and observations. To the state church, tradition is the most valuable asset, as it is the means by which national groups identify themselves culturally. This has resulted, over time, in an immunity to change.

The inert forms of most national religious groups resist even modern values that challenge the weight of religious traditions. For the sake of tradition, most national religious groups choose to continue to insist upon holding back the direction of national groups intent on freeing themselves from religious traditions that they have come to see as burdens upon private choices. Whereas this direction has nothing to do with eternal processes and divine imperatives, it illustrates the current dilemma of religion, which has pinned its hopes for its hegemony of people groups on co-opting their culture through the infusion of religious influences.

The people of God should expect changes as eternal purposes unfold in the context of time. It was common for the early apostles, as well as the people, to observe the unmistakable changes in their time and to refer back to prophecies spoken centuries before as their point of reference to understand and interpret the phenomena they were currently observing.

It is frequently reported in Scripture that persons in the New Testament, whether as individuals or as a council, would say, "This is that which was spoken by the prophets."[231] In order to come to that conclusion, they had to measure and weigh the events unfolding before their eyes in light of what had been previously declared prophetically. They judged these defining events of their times, not by the political expediency of social value of their moment, but by eternal standards. The earth is meant to host things predestined by God to reveal His intents, known before the foundations of the world.

It is certain that God's eternal purposes will continue to unfold on the earth. In every epoch, the responsibility of the righteous in the earth is to accurately judge the unfolding of events in their day by eternal standards and to reposition themselves and their mind-sets in the unfolding will of God in their times. If they fail to do so, they will be as unenlightened as the unbelievers around them and will stumble in the darkness of their own unbelief. Whether or not believers will benefit from the knowledge of this unfolding and the economies that support these changes, will depend upon whether eternal judgment, or the desire for control and predictability, is the basis of the evaluation of the events. It is still incumbent upon the Body of Christ, at present, to accurately determine when the unfolding events upon the earth are those things spoken of in prophetic Scripture.

Eternal Judgment and the Restoration of Divine Order

Before change may occur, the present order has to be evaluated. If things have been held in place by traditions or misconceptions, and the fruit of those conclusions have long been established as inconsistent with the intent of Scripture, and the ineffectiveness of these conclusions have long been obvious, then change is mandated. However, in many cases, systems that have been developed to administer these conclusions and leaders whose positions give them a vested interest in maintaining the status quo are the least interested in changing.

Eventually, their neglect of the truth in favor of their positions begin to frustrate the people who follow them to the point where the people mentally categorize ineffective forms as simply necessary aspects of social order to provide normalcy and habitual patterns of behavior. But they do not actually believe that these forms are beneficial helps in the pursuit of God and the desire for personal righteousness. Unfortunately, though, they will often continue to pattern their lives around their participation in these forms.

It is unmistakable that in the current church culture, the vast majority of people attending church regularly do so for social reasons. It is equally apparent that their search for God, and for personal righteousness, is conducted without reference to either these institutional forms or the leaders associated with them.

If people are to find their way back to the truth and to the effective working of the power of God in their lives, these religious forms and the accompanying doctrines that form the basis of the traditions with which people identify must be removed in order to make room for the truth.

Whether by complete reviews or partial assessments of particular doctrinal positions, the present form of church has to be judged. It is neither appropriate to ignore these forms nor to continue to acquiesce to them. The standards of eternal truth must be applied and these forms, together with the leaders who are the proponents of them, must be held to the account of eternal standards.

As the review progresses, the present forms that have been discredited must be replaced by the long neglected original standards. Divine order must replace traditional order as a consequence of the application of the template of the original intent of God as restored through the process of eternal judgment.

This review should not be conducted by unskilled and immature believers. God has placed, within the Body of Christ, the gift of the apostle whose primary work is to present the order of God for the relationships within the Body.

Astonishingly, both institutions and their leaders frequently do not consider eternal standards to be of any importance. Most institutions have some form of order that is an adaptation of societal order. Typically, this form is largely based upon the collective will of the membership or the historic power of certain offices within the institution. Wherever disputes arise, matters tend to be settled in a fashion that either reflects the general will of the people, in the hope of preserving the wealth and influence of their organization, or in the protection of the institution and its operatives.

By contrast, whenever disputes arose in the early Church, the apostles used the occasion to align the believers with the order of Heaven.[232] These occasions of conflict allowed for the rapid advance of the believers' understanding of the interplay between Heaven and earth.

The mind of the Lord was further disclosed in the administrations implemented by the apostles. This process saw a transition of diverse peoples into one Holy Nation.

Among the significant issues that arose was the admission of Gentiles into the early Church.[233] Previously, the Church was composed exclusively of Jewish people. Paul's work among the Gentiles eventually forced a confrontation with the apostolic leadership in Jerusalem, requiring an apostolic council to convene to rule on the matter of whether the teachings of Jesus were applicable to the Gentiles as well and to decide whether the Kingdom of Heaven was now available to all mankind, or whether Gentiles who desired access to it were required to undergo a conversion to Judaism as a precondition to admission into the Kingdom.[234]

The apostolic council in Jerusalem reviewed the prophetic Scriptures and heard the unimpeachable testimonies of apostles such as Peter and Paul and were led by the Holy Spirit to conclude that the message of Christ was as available to the Gentiles as it had been to the Jews.

This was the point at which the early Church emerged in its fullness from the prior context of the order established through Moses for the bringing forth of Christ.[235] The tradition of Judaism had served its intended purpose to bring forth the Messiah, out of the tribe of Judah. Once Christ came, with Him came grace and truth for all mankind.

It was incumbent upon the early apostles to review the order of Moses that had served its purpose, but now, like scaffolding, that order had to be taken down and discarded. In its place, the divine order of the sons of God, together with an open invitation to all mankind, had come.

The approach to God was no longer shrouded in the mystery of types and shadows, such as the tabernacle and the law. Instead, access to the throne of God had been widely granted to everyone who sought God. The veil had been torn in two by the hand of God. A new order had come and with it a new administration.

Paul was the apostle to whom the authority to establish the Gentiles in the Kingdom of God had been chiefly given.

> *For this reason I, Paul, the prisoner of Christ Jesus for the sake of you Gentiles—Surely you have heard about the administration of God's grace that was given to me for you, that is, the mystery made known to me by revelation, as I have already written briefly. In reading this, then, you will be able to understand my insight into the mystery of Christ, which was not made known to men in other generations as it has now been revealed by the Spirit to God's holy apostles and prophets. This mystery is that through the gospel the Gentiles are heirs together with Israel, members together of one body, and sharers together in the promise in Christ Jesus. I became a servant of this gospel by the gift of God's grace given me through the working of His power* (Ephesians 3:1-7 NIV).

The removal of the old order and its replacement by the new required an eternal perspective and a procedure by which the old was set aside and replaced by the new. It also required competent judges, the apostles, to perform the juridical function of acknowledging the end of one order and the introduction of another.

The early Church habitually engaged in this practice. Among the things that characterized the life of the early Church was that "they devoted themselves to the apostles' teaching and to the fellowship, to the breaking of bread and to prayer."[236]

The gift of the apostolic imparts to all believers an equipping to be able to conduct certain levels of judgment accurately employing eternal standards.[237] Each of the five gifts contributes specific and unique impartations that equip the maturing believer to function fully in the representation of God as part of the corporate Son. The specific impartation of the apostolic brings an understanding of divine order together with the appropriate administration.

All human relationships are subject to disagreements and conflicts, and members of the Household of God are no exception. Divine order is one of the distinguishing and glorifying aspects of God's people. The ability to resolve conflicts in a way that promotes maturity among those involved in disputes is an unqualified demonstration of the functional benefits of love. Although the process is never easy, consistently applied it "yields the peaceful fruit of righteousness" for those who are trained by it.[238]

It is necessary for all believers to be exposed to the Elementary Doctrine of eternal judgment inasmuch as everyone will sooner or later be involved in serious conflicts as members of the Body of Christ. The proper stewardship of these conflicts is the indispensable and necessary element of the believers' growth and maturity.

Vengeance Is Mine

Whenever an offense has been committed that is so heinous that vengeance seems the only appropriate response, judging the matter from a human perspective may seem altogether warranted. Mankind's desire for retributive justice is well represented in its legal systems.

Retribution, however, usurps all consideration for corrective justice that has eternal value. Even the believer is tempted to default to these standards in certain circumstances in order to satisfy the human desire for retribution. In the secular legal systems, it may be the only remedy to be considered. However, among the people of God, a different standard applies. Vengeance is not a goal of divine judgment. The aim is always redemption.

An eternal point of view considers that the human is a spirit clothed in flesh, and the flesh will suffer many things, including injustices, and will eventually die. The purpose of a spirit clothed in flesh is to put the nature of God on display even in circumstances of gross injustice, permitting the wrongdoer the opportunity to see the display of the nature of God in the person wronged and, thus, be shown the greater form of human life.

God has preempted the demand for vengeance among the believers, by retaining all rights to it: "Do not take revenge, my friends, but leave room for God's wrath."[239] Nothing escapes the scrutiny and ultimate judgment of God, and everything is judged by His righteous standards. Even if a matter that cries out for redress goes untended for a long while, the intent of God is not to neglect it, but to redeem that which is subject to redemption.

> *You have heard that it was said, "Love your neighbor and hate your enemy." But I tell you: Love your enemies and pray for those who persecute you, that you may be sons of your Father in heaven. He causes his sun to rise on the evil and the good, and sends rain on the righteous and the unrighteous. If you love those who love you, what reward will you get? Are not even the tax collectors doing that? And if you greet only your brothers, what are you doing more than others? Do not even pagans do that? Be perfect, therefore, as your heavenly Father is perfect* (Matthew 5:43-48 NIV).

Eventually, everyone must stand before the throne of God, the seat of eternal judgment, to give an account for his deeds.[240]

Eternal Judgment

The purposes of God may not be apparent at the time of the misdeeds of men, as in the case of Paul and Peter. The righteous judge is restrained by God's preemption of vengeance.

> *Do not take revenge, my friends, but leave room for God's wrath, for it is written: "It is Mine to avenge; I will repay," says the Lord. On the contrary: "If your enemy is hungry, feed him; if he is thirsty, give him something to drink. In doing this, you will heap burning coals on his head." Do not be overcome by evil, but overcome evil with good* (Romans 12:19-21 NIV).

It is this preemption that makes way for the Lord's will in righteous judgment.

The love of God is defined as patient, kind, and long-suffering.[241] He permits the maximum possibility of change by permitting the unrighteous to display the hidden wickedness within their hearts, so that if they could be turned, they would be induced to do so.

Suffering, whether by one's own misconduct or at the hands of the wicked, permits the victim to display the characteristics of the love of God. Whether one suffers or lives an uneventful life, all human life is characterized by its brevity.

As discussed earlier, under the Elementary Doctrine of the resurrection of the dead, it is to be understood that the human body is merely the housing for a person's indestructible spirit. All suffering in the flesh, of whatever kind, is meant to illicit a response that displays the nature of God in the face of injustice. All manner of harm relates only to the human body and is useful to perfect the responses of the human soul, while being incapable of affecting the human spirit.

Although God is patient, kind, and long-suffering, He is never tolerant of evil. God Himself is kind and merciful to all, because "[He is] not willing that any should perish, but that all should come to repentance."[242] However, God's mercy eventually gives way to His justice, when one's heart becomes sufficiently hardened that He moves beyond the point of redemption.

Even though the average person does not consider himself a wrongdoer, in the eyes of God "all have sinned and fall short of the glory of God," and "the wages of sin is death, but the gift of God is eternal life in Christ Jesus our Lord."[243] Although God's justice may be long-delayed, and individuals may be given over progressively to a "reprobate mind" by the removal of restraint, God intends to show the true nature of man's depravity as the last act of confronting him with the need to change.[244]

Even the procedures that are designed to arrest the misconduct of a brother, up to and including expelling the immoral brother, are meant to be acts of redemption.[245] However, even if it appears that the wrongdoer has managed to avoid the consequences of his illicit and wicked acts, there awaits for him a time of reckoning from which there is no escape: "If we deliberately keep on sinning after we have received the knowledge of the truth, no sacrifice for sins is left, but only a fearful expectation of judgment and of raging fire that will consume the enemies of God."[246]

Eternal judgment must be distinguished from the vengeance of God. Eternal judgment is an Elementary Doctrine with which believers must become experienced. It is part of the routine practice of every maturing believer. It is a requirement for aligning one's self with the will of God during the course of one's life, and it is a prerequisite for determining the seasons of God.

The vengeance of God—which is certain to come upon the wicked and the unbelieving—is the final decree of God over those who live in opposition to His will and purpose. The character of this judgment is in the nature of vengeance as God eventually removes the taint of sin from creation. Even angels are subject to this judgment.

Judging Angels

Do you not know that we will judge angels? How much more the things of this life! (1 Corinthians 6:3 NIV)

Eternal Judgment

As sons of God are brought to maturity, they exercise eternal judgment as the principle component of their rule over the various spheres of authority to which they are given. Unlike earthly princes, who rule by human standards, Jesus did only what He saw His Father doing, and this template remains the standard for righteous judgment among the sons of God. Whereas for individuals, this standard is applied within the spheres of rule that mature sons possess; the corporate Son also rules by this standard.

One of the prophetic utterances indicating the overall purposes of Christ coming into the world recognizes that He comes to rule as the King over the Kingdom of Heaven.[247] He established the Kingdom of Heaven and entrusted the ongoing rule of it to the Body of Christ; "The Government shall be upon His shoulders."[248] As the Head, however, He continues to exercise dominion and rule over the whole earth from His place upon the throne of God. His Body in the earth is the instrument through which He exercises His sovereign authority.

All of the activities of rule associated with the Kingdom of Heaven are designed to bring eternal standards to bear on human circumstances. As earlier noted, this process replaces the culture of sin with a heavenly culture of righteousness. The existence of the sons of God employing the authority and rule of Christ establishes the culture of the Kingdom of Heaven upon the earth.

This has the effect of challenging the model of life that has evolved out of the kingdom of darkness. The light and glory of the Kingdom of Heaven, projected through the rule of sons, has, among its effects, the ability to reclaim mankind for God and to do so by "destroying the works of the devil."[249]

God intends not only to judge and destroy Satan's works by revealing the corporate Christ and the glory of His governance; He also means to bring to judgment the angels who sinned and, ultimately, to eliminate them from the created world as part of His intent to purge the taint of sin from both the visible and the invisible creation. To understand the purpose of the judging of angels, it is necessary to understand why God created the world.

One of God's great purposes in creating the world and putting mankind into it was to permit the vindication of the righteousness of God in the choice of man as His heirs. God originally conceived of putting His love on display though the model of father and son.

> God created man as an expression of Himself that was intended to reside in a venue different from His own. The context for God's decision to make man in His own image and likeness was "so that they may rule over the fish in the sea and the birds in the sky, over the livestock and all the wild animals, and over all the creatures that move along the ground." Gen 1:26. This is consistent with God's intent to relate to man as a son and His representative, but shows that the sons' representation was to take place on the earth.[250]

The expression of God's love is displayed in its perfection in this model. God originally conceived of man as a creature who would be endowed with a spirit out of the person of God, and therefore, man would be capable of loving both God and his fellowman in the same manner in which God Himself loves.

Man was created to love as God loves and, therefore, to put the essential nature of God on display in creation. "A new command I give you: Love one another. As I have loved you, so you must love one another." [251] The standard of love in this commandment is the same standard for God and man.

By contrast, angels were created to serve both God and man.

> *For to which of the angels did God ever say, "You are My Son; today I have become your Father"? Or again, "I will be his Father, and he will be My Son"? ... Are not all angels ministering spirits sent to serve those who will inherit salvation?* (Hebrews 1:5,14 NIV)

The angels who rebelled considered that they had been unjustly relegated to serving man whom they regarded as an inferior being.[252] They wanted to be the sons and heirs of God. Because they were not created to carry and portray the love of God, their view of inheritance was related to the exercise of power rather than the restraint of love.[253]

Some of the angels, under the leadership of Lucifer, called into question God's righteousness in His choice of man as His heirs. Although God could have obliterated the angels who sinned, He understood the nature of their challenge and chose to pursue them through righteous judgment.

Had He simply annihilated them, the issues regarding the righteousness of His decision to eliminate His opposition would have been left unanswered. Alternatively, had He given them an answer, He would have lowered Himself to the same plane of created beings and empowered the creation to judge its Creator. This would have replaced divine order with chaos and eliminated all standards of righteous judgment.

Instead, He elected to provide an answer through the very creatures who were the subject of the dispute. God's answer would be that man would put on display the righteousness of God and, by that, destroy Satan's deception and hold all the angels who sinned to account. Man's righteousness as a mature son of God would put on display the exact nature of God, his Father, and become the standard for judgment of the angels themselves.

The first man, Adam, was provided the choice of relying upon the presence of God or the tree of the knowledge of good and evil as the basis of his decision-making, and he chose independence from God. He was aided in this choice by the active participation of Satan.

Jesus, the Last Adam, was subject to the same temptation to proceed by the wisdom of convenience. Instead, though hungry from forty days of fasting, He chose to feast upon the Bread of God's presence. His decision restored to man the right to live again in the presence of God.

The effective consequence of Jesus's decision was to permit mankind to be redeemed from Adam's departure and to be reassembled as the sons of God. This collection of God's children in the earth is referred to as the Body of Christ. They are to become practiced in the exercise of eternal judgment. Their affinity for this way of life will conform them to the very standards of eternal judgment and will not only destroy the devil's works, but will also be the standard by which all the angels that sinned will be held to account.

As a Holy Nation, composed of a people drawn from the entire spectrum of humanity, assembled to carry the glory of God in the earth, one of the most brilliant and startling aspects of the corporate life will be the fashion of its rule. In this regard, especially, the House of God will be seen as a city of light upon a hill. It will be the visible expression of righteousness and will be the characteristic most frequently referred to as the basis of their observably peaceful existence.

Beyond establishing righteous process in the earth, the people of God will become the standards of eternal rectitude by which the conduct of angels will be subject to the review of God's judgments.

CHAPTER SEVEN
THE ELEMENTARY DOCTRINES AND THE MATURING SON

The Elementary Doctrines both identify aspects of the culture of the corporate Son and provide the means by which that culture is established in every believer. This process is inextricably tied to the concept of maturity.

Specifically, the stages of the maturing son of God depend upon the working of the Elementary Doctrines in a believer's daily life. Scripture identifies these stages of sonship as a means of identifying one's maturity level within the range of an infant son to one who has reached his or her full representation of God the Father within the greater Body. Similarly, the stages of sonship may describe the maturing of the corporate Son, the Body of Christ, as the Body matures through new revelation across epochs of time.

Stages of Sonship

The stages of sonship begin with the infant, or newly born-again believer, and progress to the mature son. Each stage refers to a particular Greek term for "son," its meaning, and the manner in which it is used in Scripture.

The Elementary Doctrines

The infant son, or earliest stage, is called the *nēpios* stage.[254] When one is first born again, that person is a son of God and, therefore, an heir in the house of God. However, the *nēpios*, though an heir, "does not differ at all from a slave although he is owner of everything."[255]

The newborn believer is like an heir under guardianship. Such an heir is not sufficiently trained or mature enough to have free access to the resources of the household, though he is heir to everything in it. Regarding the teaching and training of the *nēpios*, that person is ready only for "milk," which is described in Scripture as the opposite of "a message of wisdom among the mature."[256]

> *For though by this time you ought to be teachers, you have need again for someone to teach you the elementary principles of the oracles of God, and you have come to need milk and not solid food. For everyone who partakes only of milk is not accustomed to the word of righteousness, for he is an infant* [nēpios]. *But solid food is for the mature, who because of practice have their senses trained to discern good and evil* (Hebrews 5:12-14 NASB).

One should note that the writer of Hebrews prescribes, specifically, the Elementary Doctrines as the starting place for the infant son of God and identifies the mature as one who has practiced them.

Paul also equated the message for those in this infantile state as preaching "nothing … except Jesus Christ, and Him crucified," and that this message is in contrast to a message of wisdom for the mature.[257] The *nēpios* stage is one in which great learning and foundation are necessary, but one in which the individual does not freely or intentionally access the resources of the House of God for lack of maturity.

The next stage of sonship is the *paidion* stage, often translated in Scripture as a child or children (pl.). John writes,

> *I am writing to you, fathers, because you know Him who has been from the beginning. I am writing to you, young*

men [neaniskos], *because you have overcome the evil one. I have written to you, children* [paidion], *because you know the Father* (1 John 2:13 NASB).

A *paidion* is a young child. In Scripture, the term is used for one who is able to recognize the Father. This stage may be considered the second stage of sonship as it is at times synonymous with a child who is an infant.[258]

The *teknon* stage comes next, and it is the first stage in which the son is sufficiently mature to be given responsibility and the opportunity to respond to rule. In terms of maturity, the *teknon* is still considered a child.[259] In terms of sonship, however, the *teknon* is a son who is sufficiently mature to engage a reciprocal relationship with the Father.

Jesus told the following parable, which involves sons who are in the *teknon* stage of maturity:

> "…A man had two sons, and he came to the first and said, 'Son, go work today in the vineyard.' And he answered, 'I will not'; but afterward he regretted it and went. The man came to the second and said the same thing; and he answered, 'I will, sir'; but he did not go. Which of the two did the will of his father?" They said, "The first." Jesus said to them, "Truly I say to you that the tax collectors and prostitutes will get into the kingdom of God before you" (Matthew 21:28-31 NASB).

These sons are of sufficient maturity to be given rule and responsibility but whose inconsistencies in carrying out the will of their father show that more training is necessary before they are sons who are the complete representation of the father.

The next stage, the *neaniskos* stage, is similar to the maturity of "young men":

> *I am writing to you, fathers, because you know Him who has been from the beginning. I am writing to you, young*

men [neaniskos], because you have overcome the evil one. I have written to you, children, because you know the Father. I have written to you, fathers, because you know Him who has been from the beginning. I have written to you, young men [neaniskos], because you are strong, and the word of God abides in you, and you have overcome the evil one. Do not love the world nor the things in the world. If anyone loves the world, the love of the Father is not in him (1 John 2:13-15 NASB).

This is the stage of the overcomer. It is a son who has been tested and displayed strength, and who, in the testing, has represented the word of God. The *neaniskos* is no longer a child, and the implication of overcoming the evil one indicates one who has been refined greatly through suffering.

The final stage of sonship is *huios*. This is the son who may be sent as the full, complete representation of the Father. Perhaps the most important distinction of the *huios* in Scripture follows the parable described above of the man with two, *teknon*, sons, when Jesus tells the following parable:

"…There was a landowner who PLANTED A VINEYARD AND PUT A WALL AROUND IT AND DUG A WINE PRESS IN IT, AND BUILT A TOWER, and rented it out to vine-growers and went on a journey. When the harvest time approached, he sent his slaves to the vine-growers to receive his produce. The vine-growers took his slaves and beat one, and killed another, and stoned a third. Again he sent another group of slaves larger than the first; and they did the same thing to them. But afterward he sent his son [huios] *to them, saying, 'They will respect my son.' But when the vine-growers saw the son, they said among themselves, 'This is the heir; come, let us kill him and seize his inheritance.' They took him, and threw*

him out of the vineyard and killed him. Therefore when the owner of the vineyard comes, what will he do to those vine-growers?" They said to Him, "He will bring those wretches to a wretched end, and will rent out the vineyard to other vine-growers who will pay him the proceeds at the proper seasons." Jesus said to them, "Did you never read in the Scriptures, 'THE STONE WHICH THE BUILDERS REJECTED, THIS BECAME THE CHIEF CORNER stone; THIS CAME ABOUT FROM THE LORD, AND IT IS MARVELOUS IN OUR EYES'? Therefore I say to you, the kingdom of God will be taken away from you and given to a people, producing the fruit of it. And he who falls on this stone will be broken to pieces; but on whomever it falls, it will scatter him like dust" (Matthew 21:33-44 NASB).

The Son in the parable references Christ, the Son who was sent. This Son's representation of the Father is so complete that He may be knowingly sent into harm or death and that such harm is itself an indictment against those who would reject him.

The *huios* son carries a measure of the House of God when he is sent, establishing the standards of righteousness by his representation of the Father. This is the fully mature, Christ-like son.

Repentance, Faith Toward God, Baptisms, the Laying On of Hands, the Resurrection of the Dead, and *Eternal Judgment* are the principles upon which maturity is built in each believer as he or she progresses from an infant to a son who is sent as a dispensation of God's House.

These teachings form the basis of how each person may be raised in the Family of God to reflect its culture. It is from these building blocks that both the individual and the corporate Son progress from salvation to the exact representation of the Father, by which the rest of the world can see God's invisible qualities put on display through His Son.

ENDNOTES

1. See Galatians 3:25-29 NIV; see also Romans 8:15-17 NIV.
2. Hebrews 6:1b-2 NIV.
3. Hebrews 6:1b NIV.
4. John 1:12b KJV.
5. See Galatians 3:26-28 NIV: "You are all sons of God through faith in Christ Jesus. ... There is neither Jew nor Greek, slave nor free, male nor female, for you are all one in Christ Jesus."
6. See Romans 8:14 NIV. (In his letter to the Romans, Paul wrote that "those who are led by the Spirit of God are sons of God," referring to a son in the *huios* stage, which is one who is a mature son, fit to represent the Father; see Strong's G5207, *huios*.)
7. First Corinthians 2:2 NIV.
8. First Corinthians 3:1-2 NIV.
9. Romans 8:5 NIV.
10. See, e.g., Matthew 26:38,41 NIV: "My soul is overwhelmed with sorrow to the point of death. Stay here and keep watch with Me. ... Watch and pray so that you will not fall into temptation. The spirit is willing, but the body is weak."

The Elementary Doctrines

11. See First Thessalonians 5:23 NIV: "May God Himself, the God of peace, sanctify you through and through. May your whole spirit, soul and body be kept blameless at the coming of our Lord Jesus Christ."

12. See Genesis 2:7 NIV.

13. See, e.g., Romans 8:16 NIV: "The Spirit Himself testifies with our spirit that we are God's children."; see also Hebrews 10:15-16 NIV: "The Holy Spirit also testifies to us about this. First He says: 'This is the covenant I will make with them after that time, says the Lord. I will put My laws in their hearts, and I will write them on their minds.'"

14. James 3:15 KJV.

15. Romans 8:6-7 NIV.

16. See Romans 6:23 NIV: "For the wages of sin is death, but the gift of God is eternal life in Christ Jesus our Lord."; see Romans 8:2 NIV "[T]hrough Christ Jesus the law of the Spirit of life set me free from the law of sin and death."

17. Ephesians 2:4b-5 NIV.

18. See Romans 6:1b-7 NIV: "Shall we go on sinning so that grace may increase? By no means! We died to sin; how can we live in it any longer? Or don' you know that all of us who were baptized into Christ Jesus were baptized into His death? ...because anyone who has died has been freed from sin."

19. First John 2:16b KJV.

20. See John 3:6 NIV: "Flesh gives birth to flesh, but the Spirit gives birth to spirit."

21. Second Corinthians 5:18-19a NIV.

22. Romans 6:23 NIV.

23. See Hebrews 12:9 NIV: "Moreover, we have all had human fathers who disciplined us and we respected them for it. How much more should we submit to the Father of our spirits and

live!"; also see Romans 8:14 NIV: "[B]ecause those who are led by the Spirit of God are sons of God."; also see John 1:12-13 NIV: "Yet to all who received Him, to those who believed in His name, He gave the right to become children of God—children born not of natural descent, nor of human decision or a husband's will, but born of God."

24. See Luke 3:38 NIV: "…Adam, the son of God."

25. See Hebrews 1:5,14 NIV: "For to which of the angels did God ever say, 'You are My Son; today I have become your Father'? Or again, 'I will be his Father, and he will be My Son'? … Are not all angels ministering spirits sent to serve those who will inherit salvation?"

26. Genesis 3:19 NIV.

27. See Matthew 12:43-45 NIV; also see Luke 11:24-26 NIV.

28. See Sam Soleyn with Nicholas Soleyn, *My Father! My Father!* (2012) for a full discussion of the role of spiritual fathers.

29. First John 2:14 NIV.

30. Hebrews 5:12,14 NIV.

31. Colossians 1:15,22 NIV.

32. See John chapter 14 NIV.

33. Hebrews 11:6 NIV.

34. Matthew 4:4b NIV.

35. Jeremiah 1:5 NIV.

36. John 18:37b NIV.

37. See Genesis 37:5-10 NIV.

38. Galatians 1:15; see also verse 16 NIV.

39. For a more detailed discussion of this culture, refer to *My Father! My Father!* by Sam Soleyn and Nicholas Soleyn.

40. See John 6:28b-29 NIV: "'What must we do to do the works God requires?' Jesus answered, 'The work of God is this: to believe in the One He has sent.'"

41. Hebrews 1:3 NIV.

42. John 7:18 NIV.

43. John 7:16-17 NIV.

44. Hebrews 11:1 KJV.

45. See Hebrews 11:3 NIV.

46. Id.; Hebrews 2:7,9 NIV, showing that mankind was made "a little lower than the angels."

47. Matthew 12:28 NIV; see also Luke 9:1 NIV: "When Jesus had called the Twelve together, He gave them power and authority to drive out all demons and to cure diseases."

48. See John 3:16 NIV: "For God so loved the world that He gave His one and only Son, that whoever believes in Him shall not perish but have eternal life."

49. Webster's Third New International Dictionary, Unabridged, "economy." (Merriam-Webster, 2002; available at http://unabridged.merriam-webster.com; June 8, 2012.)

50. See Genesis 3:19 NIV: God identifying mankind's new economy, saying, "By the sweat of your brow you will eat your food until you return to the ground, since from it you were taken; for dust you are and to dust you will return."

51. See Matthew 4:4 NIV: "…Man does not live on bread alone, but on every word that comes from the mouth of God."

52. See Hebrews 11:3 NIV.

53. Second Corinthians 4:18 NIV.

54. Second Corinthians 4:3-18 NIV.

Endnotes

55. See Psalm 8:5 NIV: "You made Him a little lower than the heavenly beings and crowned Him with glory and honor."; see also Hebrews 2:7,9 NIV: "You made Him a little lower than the angels; you crowned Him with glory and honor. … But we see Jesus, who was made a little lower than the angels, now crowned with glory and honor because He suffered death, so that by the grace of God He might taste death for everyone."

56. See Second Corinthians 12:2 NIV: "I know a man in Christ who fourteen years ago was caught up to the third heaven. Whether it was in the body or out of the body I do not know—God knows."

57. See Isaiah 14:12-14 NIV: "How you have fallen from heaven, O morning star, son of the dawn! You have been cast down to the earth, you who once laid low the nations! You said in your heart, 'I will ascend to heaven; I will raise my throne above the stars of God; I will sit enthroned on the mount of assembly, on the utmost heights of the sacred mountain. I will ascend above the tops of the clouds; I will make myself like the Most High.'"; see also Matthew 24:29 NIV, referencing "heavenly bodies" as being shaken.

58. See Ephesians 6:12 NIV: "For our struggle is not against flesh and blood, but against the rulers, against the authorities, against the powers of this dark world and against the spiritual forces of evil in the heavenly realms."

59. See Job 1:6-7 NIV: "One day the angels came to present themselves before the Lord, and Satan also came with them. The Lord said to Satan, 'Where have you come from?' Satan answered the Lord, 'From roaming through the earth and going back and forth in it.'"

60. See Luke 22:31 NIV: "Simon, Simon, Satan has asked to sift you as wheat."

61. See Matthew 12:28 NIV.

62. See Matthew 26:39 NIV: "…He fell with His face to the ground and prayed, 'My Father, if it is possible, may this cup be taken from Me. Yet not as I will, but as You will.'"

63. John 5:19b NIV.

64. See Matthew 21:2-3 NIV: "Go to the village ahead of you, and at once you will find a donkey tied there, with her colt by her. Untie them and bring them to Me. If anyone says anything to you, tell him that the Lord needs them, and he will send them right away," fulfilling Zechariah 9:9 NIV.

65. See Hebrews 6:2 NIV.

66. See Acts 10:44-48a NIV: "While Peter was still speaking these words, the Holy Spirit came on all who heard the message. … 'Can anyone keep these people from being baptized with water? They have received the Holy Spirit just as we have.' So he ordered that they be baptized in the name of Jesus Christ."; see also Acts 11:15-17 NIV.

67. See Acts 2:38,41 NIV: "Peter replied, 'Repent and be baptized, every one of you, in the name of Jesus Christ for the forgiveness of your sins. And you will receive the gift of the Holy Spirit.' … Those who accepted his message were baptized, and about three thousand were added to their number that day."; see also Acts 8:15-17 NIV: "When they arrived, they prayed for them that they might receive the Holy Spirit, because the Holy Spirit had not yet come upon any of them; they had simply been baptized into the name of the Lord Jesus. Then Peter and John placed their hands on them, and they received the Holy Spirit."

68. See First Peter 4:1 NIV: "Therefore, since Christ suffered in His body, arm yourselves also with the same attitude, because he who has suffered in his body is done with sin."; see also First Peter 4:12-13 NIV: "Dear friends, do not be surprised at the painful trial you are suffering, as though something strange were happening to you. But rejoice that you participate in the

Endnotes

sufferings of Christ, so that you may be overjoyed when His glory is revealed."

69. See First Corinthians 12:13 NIV: "For we were all baptized by one Spirit into one body—whether Jews or Greeks, slave or free—and we were all given the one Spirit to drink."

70. See also John 4:1-42 NIV, relating Jesus's encounter with the Samaritan woman at the well.

71. Sam Soleyn & Nicholas Soleyn, *My Father! My Father!*, chapter 7, pp. 63-70 (2012).

72. See First John 2:15-16 KJV.

73. See Soleyn, supra, pp. 64-65, *The Kosmos* (discussing reliance on the kosmos as a substitute for relying on God).

74. See Colossians 1:13-14 NIV.

75. Second Corinthians 5:17 NIV.

76. See Ephesians 6:12 NIV: "For our struggle is not against flesh and blood, but against the rulers, against the authorities, against the powers of this dark world and against the spiritual forces of evil in the heavenly realms."

77. Romans 7:25b NIV.

78. Soleyn, supra, pp. 65-70.

79. Ephesians 6:12b KJV.

80. Romans 8:1-2 NIV.

81. See Romans 6:22-23 NIV: "But now that you have been set free from sin and have become slaves to God, the benefit you reap leads to holiness, and the result is eternal life. For the wages of sin is death, but the gift of God is eternal life in Christ Jesus our Lord."

82. See Acts 10:46-47 NIV: "For they heard them speaking in tongues and praising God. Then Peter said, 'Can anyone keep

these people from being baptized with water? They have received the Holy Spirit just as we have.'"

83. Second Corinthians 5:17b NIV.

84. First Peter 3:21 KJV.

85. See Acts 2:38,41 NIV: "Repent and be baptized, every one of you, in the name of Jesus Christ for the forgiveness of your sins. And you will receive the gift of the Holy Spirit."; see "Repentance From Acts That Lead to Death," *Elementary Doctrine Series,* May 2012; available at http://www.soleynpublishing.com/resources/.

86. See First John 2:1: "My dear children, I write this to you so that you will not sin. But if anybody does sin, we have one who speaks to the Father in our defense—Jesus Christ, the Righteous One."

87. See Matthew 3:16-17 NIV: "As soon as Jesus was baptized, He went up out of the water. At that moment heaven was opened, and He saw the Spirit of God descending like a dove and lighting on Him. And a voice from heaven said, 'This is My Son, whom I love; with Him I am well pleased.'"; see also Acts 10:37-38 NIV: "You know what has happened throughout Judea, beginning in Galilee after the baptism that John preached—how God anointed Jesus of Nazareth with the Holy Spirit and power, and how He went around doing good and healing all who were under the power of the devil, because God was with Him."

88. See First Corinthians 12:1 NIV: "Now about spiritual gifts, brothers, I do not want you to be ignorant."

89. See First Corinthians 12:11-12 NIV: "All these are the work of one and the same Spirit, and He gives them to each one, just as He determines. The body is a unit, though it is made up of many parts; and though all its parts are many, they form one body. So it is with Christ."

Endnotes

90. Matthew 28:18 NIV.
91. See Matthew 28:19-20 NIV: "Therefore go and make disciples of all nations, baptizing them in the name of the Father and of the Son and of the Holy Spirit, and teaching them to obey everything I have commanded you. And surely I am with you always, to the very end of the age."
92. See First Thessalonians 1:5a NIV: "Because our gospel came to you not simply with words, but also with power, with the Holy Spirit and with deep conviction."
93. Matthew 28:18 NIV.
94. Matthew 3:11 NIV; see also Mark 1:8; Luke 3:16; John 1:33 NIV.
95. Acts 1:4-5 NIV.
96. Acts 1:8 NIV.
97. See Matthew 28:19-20 NIV, instructing the disciples that Jesus's plenary authority would accompany them in their Great Commission.
98. First Corinthians 12:31 NIV.
99. See Acts 2:37-43 NIV: "When the people heard this, they were cut to the heart and said to Peter and the other apostles, 'Brothers, what shall we do?' ... Those who accepted his message were baptized, and about three thousand were added to their number that day. ... Everyone was filled with awe, and many wonders and miraculous signs were done by the apostles."
100. See Romans 11:29 NIV: "For God's gifts and His call are irrevocable."
101. See First Corinthians 12:29-31 NIV.
102. See Ephesians 4:8,11-12 NKJV: "Therefore He says: 'When He ascended on high, He led captivity captive, and gave gifts [*domas*] to men.' ... And He Himself gave some to be apostles, some prophets, some evangelists, and some pastors and teach-

ers, for the equipping of the saints for the work of ministry, for the edifying of the body of Christ."

103. Ephesians 4:14 NIV.

104. One may find additional material for studying spiritual gifts in Sam's *Government of God* series, Programs 47-57, available at: http://www.soleyn.com/download_materials.html/.

105. See Acts 2:38 NIV: "Repent and be baptized, every one of you, in the name of Jesus Christ for the forgiveness of your sins. And you will receive the gift of the Holy Spirit."

106. Genesis 3:19 NIV.

107. See Chapter 2, "Faith Toward God," the section entitled "The Economy of the Spirit," pages 31-33.

108. See Chapter 1, "Repentance From Acts That Lead to Death."

109. See Chapter 2, "Faith Toward God" (page 25); "A son of God will reveal God's invisible qualities in the life that God has articulated to him or her."

110. See Ephesians 4:16 KJV: "From [Christ] the whole body fitly joined together and compacted by that which every joint supplieth, according to the effectual working in the measure of every part, maketh increase of the body unto the edifying of itself in love."

111. See Chapter 1, "Repentance From Acts That Lead To Death."

112. See Chapter 2, "Faith Toward God."

113. John 3:5-7 NIV.

114. See Psalm 2:2 NIV; see also Acts 4:26 NIV.

115. See Romans 12:1 NIV: "Therefore, I urge you, brothers, in view of God's mercy, to offer your bodies as living sacrifices, holy and pleasing to God—this is your spiritual act of worship."

116. Soleyn and Soleyn, *My Father! My Father!*, supra p. 139.

Endnotes

117. See Matthew 3:11; Luke 3:16b NIV: "He will baptize you with the Holy Spirit and with fire."

118. Soleyn and Soleyn, supra, p. 95.

119. See Romans 8:13-16 NIV: "…The Spirit Himself testifies with our spirit that we are God's children."

120. Romans 8:14 NIV (emphasis added).

121. See Soleyn and Soleyn, supra, pp. 52-53, "Man's Nature."

122. Id., p. 53.

123. See Hebrews 12:7-8 NIV: " ... If you are not disciplined (and everyone undergoes discipline), then you are illegitimate children and not true sons."

124. Hebrews 12:11 NIV.

125. Hebrews 5:8-10 NIV.

126. Luke 2:49-52 KJV; see also Matthew 3:17 NIV: "This is My Son, whom I love; with Him I am well pleased."

127. Hebrews 6:1 NIV.

128. See Leviticus; see also Hebrews 5:1 NIV: "Every high priest is selected from among men and is appointed to represent them in matters related to God, to offer gifts and sacrifices for sins."

129. See Hebrews 5:4 NIV: "No one takes this honor upon himself; he must be called by God, just as Aaron was. So Christ also did not take upon Himself the glory of becoming a high priest. But God said to Him, "You are My Son; today I have become Your Father."

130. See Hebrews 5:6: "And He says in another place, 'You are a priest forever, in the order of Melchizedek.'"; see also Hebrews 6:20 NIV: "…Jesus, who went before us, has entered on our behalf. He has become a high priest forever, in the order of Melchizedek."

The Elementary Doctrines

131. See Hebrews 6:20 NIV.

132. See Deuteronomy 5:2-4 NIV.

133. Strong's G652.

134. See Strong's G32, *Angelos*, pronounced ä'n-ge-los, meaning "a messenger, envoy, one who is sent, an angel, a messenger from God."

135. See John 1:51 NIV: "I tell you the truth, you shall see heaven open, and the angels of God ascending and descending on the Son of Man."; see also Genesis 28:12 NIV: "[Jacob] had a dream in which he saw a stairway resting on the earth, with its top reaching to heaven, and the angels of God were ascending and descending on it."

136. See Daniel 10:4-10 NIV, appearing to Daniel saying he had been sent and would be required to return to Heaven.

137. See Daniel 10:13,20-21 NIV: "But the prince of the Persian kingdom resisted me twenty-one days. Then Michael, one of the chief princes, came to help me, because I was detained there with the king of Persia. ... 'Soon I will return to fight against the prince of Persia, and when I go, the prince of Greece will come; but first I will tell you what is written in the Book of Truth. (No one supports me against them except Michael, your prince.)'"

138. See Revelation 4:1 NIV: "Come up here, and I will show you what must take place after this."

139. Second Corinthians 12:2 NIV.

140. See Genesis 1:26,28 NIV: "'Let Us make man in Our image, in Our likeness, and let them rule over the fish of the sea and the birds of the air, over the livestock, over all the earth, and over all the creatures that move along the ground.' ... God blessed them and said to them, 'Be fruitful and increase in number; fill the earth and subdue it. Rule over the fish of the sea and the birds of the air and over every living creature that moves on the ground.'"

Endnotes

141. See Ephesians 1:4-5 NIV: "For He chose us in Him before the creation of the world to be holy and blameless in His sight. In love He predestined us to be adopted as His sons through Jesus Christ, in accordance with His pleasure and will."

142. See John 16:14-15 NIV: "He will bring glory to Me by taking from what is Mine and making it known to you. All that belongs to the Father is Mine. That is why I said the Spirit will take from what is Mine and make it known to you."; see also Acts 1:8 NIV: "You will receive power when the Holy Spirit comes on you; and you will be My witnesses in Jerusalem, and in all Judea and Samaria, and to the ends of the earth."; see also Romans 12:4-5 NIV: "…so in Christ we who are many form one body, and each member belongs to all the others."

143. See Matthew 8:1-13 NIV: Jesus healing the centurion's servant.

144. See Luke 4:40 NIV: "When the sun was setting, the people brought to Jesus all who had various kinds of sickness, and laying His hands on each one, He healed them."; see also Mark 8:22-25 NIV.

145. See Acts 3:7-8 NIV: "Taking him by the right hand, he helped him up, and instantly the man's feet and ankles became strong. He jumped to his feet and began to walk. Then he went with them into the temple courts, walking and jumping, and praising God."

146. See Mark 16:17 NIV: "And these signs will accompany those who believe: In My name they will drive out demons; they will speak in new tongues."; see also Acts 2:22 NIV: "Jesus of Nazareth was a man accredited by God to you by miracles, wonders and signs, which God did among you through Him, as you yourselves know."

147. See First Corinthians 2:4 NIV.

148. First Thessalonians 1:4-5 NIV.

The Elementary Doctrines

149. Matthew 12:28 NIV; see also Luke 11:20 NIV; see The Elementary Doctrines, "Faith Toward God," discussing the order of authorities.

150. See Acts chapter 3 NIV.

151. See Acts 8:1,4,6 NIV: "On that day a great persecution broke out against the church at Jerusalem, and all except the apostles were scattered throughout Judea and Samaria. ... Those who had been scattered preached the word wherever they went. ... When the crowds heard Philip and saw the miraculous signs he did, they all paid close attention to what he said."

152. First Corinthians 2:4-5 NIV.

153. See Acts 2:22 NIV.

154. See Acts 14:3 NIV: "So Paul and Barnabas spent considerable time there, speaking boldly for the Lord, who confirmed the message of His grace by enabling them to do miraculous signs and wonders."

155. See James 5:14-15 NIV: "Is any one of you sick? He should call the elders of the church to pray over him and anoint him with oil in the name of the Lord. And the prayer offered in faith will make the sick person well; the Lord will raise him up. If he has sinned, he will be forgiven."

156. See Acts 3:6 NIV: "Silver or gold I do not have, but what I have I give you. In the name of Jesus Christ of Nazareth, walk."

157. See Acts 8:17 NIV: "Then Peter and John placed their hands on them, and they received the Holy Spirit."

158. See Acts 2:2-4 NIV, describing a spontaneous occurrence of the baptism with the Spirit on the Day of Pentecost; see also Acts 10:44 NIV: "While Peter was still speaking these words, the Holy Spirit came on all who heard the message."

159. See Romans 11:1 NIV: "I long to see you so that I may impart to you some spiritual gift to make you strong."; see also First

Endnotes

Corinthians 12:4-7 NIV: "There are different kinds of gifts, but the same Spirit. There are different kinds of service, but the same Lord. There are different kinds of working, but the same God works all of them in all men. Now to each one the manifestation of the Spirit is given for the common good."

160. See Galatians 1:15-16 NIV: "But when God, who set me apart from birth and called me by His grace, was pleased to reveal His Son in me so that I might preach Him among the Gentiles, I did not consult any man."; see also Acts 9:15 NIV: "The Lord said to Ananias, 'Go! This man is My chosen instrument to carry My name before the Gentiles and their kings and before the people of Israel.'"

161. See Romans 11:1 NIV.

162. See First Corinthians 14 NIV.

163. Romans 1:11-12 NIV.

164. See First Corinthians 14:40 NIV: " Everything should be done in a fitting and orderly way."

165. See First Timothy 4:14 NIV: "Do not neglect your gift, which was given you through a prophetic message when the body of elders laid their hands on you."; see also Second Timothy 1:6 NIV: "For this reason I remind you to fan into flame the gift of God, which is in you through the laying on of my hands."

166. See Galatians 1:15-17 NIV; Romans 11:29 NIV: "God's gifts and His call are irrevocable."

167. See First Thessalonians 1:1; 2:6 NIV.

168. See Acts 16:1-2 NIV.

169. See First Timothy 4:14 NIV.

170. See First Timothy 2:6 NIV.

171. See Acts 14:21-22 KJV: "They returned again to Lystra, and to Iconium, and Antioch, confirming the souls of the disciples,

and exhorting them to continue in the faith, and that we must through much tribulation enter into the kingdom of God."

172. See Acts chapter 13 NIV.
173. See Acts 11:25-26 NIV.
174. See Second Timothy 2:6 NIV.
175. Genesis 1:11 KJV.
176. John 12:24 NIV.
177. See John 11:25 NIV.
178. Soleyn and Soleyn, *My Father! My Father!,* p. 42 (2012).
179. See John 3:6-7 NIV.
180. Genesis 8:22 NIV (emphasis added).
181. John 11:25-26 NIV.
182. Luke 3:38 NIV.
183. Soleyn and Soleyn, *My Father! My Father!* p. 53 (2012).
184. Soleyn and Soleyn, supra, p. 75.
185. Id.
186. Id.
187. "On the Morning of Christ's Nativity" (1629).
188. First Corinthians 12:11-12 NIV.
189. See Ephesians 5:23 NIV: "For the husband is the head of the wife as Christ is the head of the church, His body, of which He is the Savior."; see also Romans 12:5; First Corinthians 12:12-13,27 NIV.
190. Acts 2:22 NIV.
191. Acts 2:24,32,36 NIV.
192. See First Corinthians 15:42-44 NIV.

Endnotes

193. First Corinthians 15:17-19 NIV.

194. John 11:25-26 NIV.

195. See Romans 8:15-17 NIV: "For you did not receive a spirit that makes you a slave again to fear, but you received the Spirit of sonship. And by Him we cry, 'Abba, Father.' The Spirit Himself testifies with our spirit that we are God's children. Now if we are children, then we are heirs—heirs of God and co-heirs with Christ, if indeed we share in His sufferings in order that we may also share in His glory."

196. See John 17:5 NIV: "And now, Father, glorify Me in Your presence with the glory I had with You before the world began."

197. See John 14:6-7 NIV: "Jesus answered, 'I am the way and the truth and the life. No one comes to the Father except through Me. If you really knew Me, you would know My Father as well. From now on, you do know Him and have seen Him.'"

198. Colossians 1:12 NIV.

199. John 3:6-7 NIV.

200. See Romans 8:11 NIV: "And if the Spirit of Him who raised Jesus from the dead is living in you, He who raised Christ from the dead will also give life to your mortal bodies through His Spirit, who lives in you."

201. First Corinthians 13:11 NIV; see also First Corinthians 3:1-3 NIV: "Brothers, I could not address you as spiritual but as worldly—mere infants in Christ. I gave you milk, not solid food, for you were not yet ready for it. Indeed, you are still not ready. You are still worldly. For since there is jealousy and quarreling among you, are you not worldly? Are you not acting like mere men?"

202. See First John 5:11b-12 NIV: "God has given us eternal life, and this life is in His Son. He who has the Son has life; he who does not have the Son of God does not have life."

203. See First Thessalonians 4:14-17.
204. Matthew 24:3 et seq. NIV; see also First Thessalonians 4:14-17 supra.
205. See Acts 1:10-11 NIV.
206. See Romans 6:22-23 NIV: "But now that you have been set free from sin and have become slaves to God, the benefit you reap leads to holiness, and the result is eternal life. For the wages of sin is death, but the gift of God is eternal life in Christ Jesus our Lord."; Soleyn and Soleyn, *The Elementary Doctrines Study Series*, "Baptisms" p. 9 (2012).
207. First Corinthians 15:35 NIV.
208. See Matthew 10:28 NIV: "Do not be afraid of those who kill the body but cannot kill the soul. Rather, be afraid of the One who can destroy both soul and body in hell."
209. See also Hebrews 4:12 NIV: "For the word of God is alive and active. Sharper than any double-edged sword, it penetrates even to dividing soul and spirit, joints and marrow; it judges the thoughts and attitudes of the heart."
210. Romans 8:14 NIV.
211. See Judges 17:6 KJV: "In those days Israel had no king; everyone did as he saw fit."
212. See Second Thessalonians 2:2-4 NIV: "[Do not] become easily unsettled or alarmed by some prophecy, report or letter supposed to have come from us, saying that the day of the Lord has already come. Don't let anyone deceive you in any way, for that day will not come until the rebellion occurs and the man of lawlessness is revealed, the man doomed to destruction. He will oppose and will exalt himself over everything that is called God or is worshiped, so that he sets himself up in God's temple, proclaiming himself to be God."

Endnotes

213. See John 13:34 NIV, establishing this standard through the central commandment of the New Covenant, "As I have loved you, so you must love one another."
214. See Matthew 6:1-5 NIV supra.
215. Matthew 18:18 NIV.
216. See Acts 7:58, 8:1 NIV: "[They] dragged [Stephen] out of the city and began to stone him. Meanwhile, the witnesses laid their clothes at the feet of a young man named Saul. ... And Saul was consenting unto his death."
217. See Matthew 26:69-75 NIV.
218. See John 21:17 NIV.
219. See Matthew 16:17-19 NIV: "Blessed are you, Simon son of Jonah, for this was not revealed to you by man, but by My Father in heaven. And I tell you that you are Peter, and on this rock I will build My church, and the gates of Hades will not overcome it. I will give you the keys of the kingdom of heaven; whatever you bind on earth will be bound in heaven, and whatever you loose on earth will be loosed in heaven."; see also Acts 2 and Acts 10.
220. Matthew 7:6 NIV.
221. See John 12:47-48 NIV: "As for the person who hears My words but does not keep them, I do not judge him. For I did not come to judge the world, but to save it. There is a judge for the one who rejects Me and does not accept My words; that very word which I spoke will condemn him at the last day."; see also First Corinthians 6:1-11 supra.
222. See Acts 15 NIV, judging of matters concerning the entire Church; see also Acts 5:1-10 NIV, showing Peter's judgment over personal matters.
223. See Galatians 6:7-10 NIV: "Do not be deceived: God cannot be mocked. A man reaps what he sows. The one who sows to

please his sinful nature, from that nature will reap destruction; the one who sows to please the Spirit, from the Spirit will reap eternal life. Let us not become weary in doing good, for at the proper time we will reap a harvest if we do not give up. Therefore, as we have opportunity, let us do good to all people, especially to those who belong to the family of believers."

224. See Matthew 4:1-4 NIV.

225. Matthew 4:4 NIV (quoting Deuteronomy 8:3).

226. Matthew 4:6 NIV (quoting Psalm 91:11-12).

227. Matthew 4:7 NIV (quoting Deuteronomy 6:16).

228. See Matthew 18:17 NIV: "If he refuses to listen to them, tell it to the church; and if he refuses to listen even to the church, treat him as you would a pagan or a tax collector."

229. See Daniel 5:30-33 NIV; see also Daniel 10:20.

230. Revelation 1:8 NASB.

231. See Acts 1:20 NIV: "[I]t is written in the book of Psalms, 'May his place be deserted; let here be no one to dwell in it,' and, 'May another take his place of leadership.'"; see also Acts 2:16 NIV: "No, this is what was spoken by the prophet Joel."; see also Acts 3:17-18,24 NIV: "Now, brothers, I know that you acted in ignorance, as did your leaders. But this is how God fulfilled what He had foretold through all the prophets, saying that his Christ would suffer. ... Indeed, all the prophets from Samuel on, as many as have spoken, have foretold these days."

232. See Acts 6:1-4 NIV: "In those days when the number of disciples was increasing, the Grecian Jews among them complained against the Hebraic Jews because their widows were being overlooked in the daily distribution of food. So the Twelve gathered all the disciples together and said, 'It would not be right for us to neglect the ministry of the word of God in order to wait on tables. Brothers, choose seven men from among you

Endnotes

who are known to be full of the Spirit and wisdom. We will turn this responsibility over to them and will give our attention to prayer and the ministry of the word.'"; see also Acts 15:6-20 (Jerusalem Counsel).

233. See Acts chapter 15 NIV.

234. See Acts chapter 16 NIV.

235. See John 1:17 NIV: "For the law was given through Moses; grace and truth came through Jesus Christ."

236. Acts 2:42 NIV.

237. See Ephesians 4:11-13 NIV: "[So Christ Himself] gave some to be apostles, some to be prophets, some to be evangelists, and some to be pastors and teachers, to prepare God's people for works of service, so that the body of Christ may be built up until we all reach unity in the faith and in the knowledge of the Son of God and become mature, attaining to the whole measure of the fullness of Christ."

238. See Hebrews 12:11 NASB.

239. Romans 12:19a NIV; see also Hebrews 10:30-31 NIV: "For we know Him who said, 'It is Mine to avenge; I will repay,' and again, 'The Lord will judge His people.' It is a dreadful thing to fall into the hands of the living God."; see also Deuteronomy 32:35-36 NIV.

240. See Second Corinthians 5:10 NIV: "For we must all appear before the judgment seat of Christ, so that each one may receive what is due him for the things done while in the body, whether good or bad."

241. See First Corinthians 13:4 NIV.

242. Second Peter 3:9b KJV.

243. Romans 3:23; 6:23 NIV.

244. See Romans 1:28,32 KJV; see also Second Timothy 3:8-9 KJV.

245. See Matthew 18:15; First Corinthians 5:9-12 NIV.

246. Hebrews 10:26-27 NIV; see also Hebrews 10:30-31 NIV: "For we know Him who said, 'It is Mine to avenge; I will repay,' and again, 'The Lord will judge His people.' It is a dreadful thing to fall into the hands of the living God."

247. See Isaiah 9:6-7 NIV.

248. Id.

249. See First John 3:8 NIV: "He who does what is sinful is of the devil, because the devil has been sinning from the beginning. The reason the Son of God appeared was to destroy the devil's work."

250. Soleyn and Soleyn, *My Father! My Father!*, Ch. 6, p. 57 (2012).

251. See John 13:34 NIV.

252. See Hebrews 2:6-9 NIV: discussing mankind as being made "a little lower than the angels."

253. See Galatians 4:7 NIV: "So you are no longer a slave, but a son; and since you are a son, God has made you also an heir."

254. See Strong's G3516, *nēpios*, "(1) an infant, little child; (2) a minor, not of age; (3) metaph. childish, untaught, unskilled."

255. Galatians 4:1 NASB.

256. See First Corinthians 2:6 NASB.

257. See First Corinthians 2:1-7 NASB; see also First Corinthians 3:1 NASB.

258. Strong's G3813.

259. See First John 2:12 NASB: "I am writing to you, little children [*teknion*], because your sins have been forgiven you for His name's sake."

My Father! My Father!

SAM SOLEYN
WITH
NICHOLAS SOLEYN

In the Kingdom of God, each person's destiny is the playing out of that person's unique identity as a son of God, regardless of gender, race, or background. To embrace one's identity as a son, one must change his prevailing culture.

In this season, God is building His House in the earth, with the relationship of fathers and sons as its foundation. Effecting cultural changes requires a trans-generational effort, in which a change in the culture is but one of the first steps of a long journey to reestablish, fully, the House of God. This journey is meant to reposition man in the relationship with God as Father, as God intended from the beginning. The purpose of repositioning humankind as sons and heirs to God is to establish the family of God on the earth and to display the love of God, through his sons, to all of creation. Whereas the destiny of each son of God is vitally important, the entire purpose of God can only, ultimately, be accomplished through the corporate form—the House of God.

AVAILABLE FOR PURCHASE AT....

eGenCo

WWW.EGEN.CO | INFO@EGEN.CO | 717.461.3436

The Removal of RESTRAINT

Sam Soleyn

Those who have willingly accepted being confirmed to the will of God through their sufferings are finding themselves becoming deeply transformed, and nothing is remaining the same. They are finding their security and well being in new insights into the nature of God's character. They are discovering the spiritual reality of an entire existence based upon the reliability of the love of God, the Father. They are themselves becoming visible and accurate representations of the Invisible God. Trials and sufferings are understood to be essential parts of this process of transformation. These adversities are bringing to light the hidden areas that must be brought to accurate alignment with divine standards. A great separation has begun. It is resulting from the stark distinctions between the choices that have been made and the resulting patterns of life that flow from these radically dissimilar choices. The result will come to be clear and unmistakable: "The wicked are wicked still, and the righteous are righteous still."

Two final results of the removal of restraint will ultimately war with each other. One will be that all divine standards are rejected in favor of a view of God that is a product of the popular secular imagination. A god created of the popular demand by the popular imagination and for the popular consumption. The other will be the mature expression of Christ appearing as a "City upon a hill." All humanity will be ultimately of one or the other condition.

AVAILABLE FOR PURCHASE AT....

eGenco

WWW.EGEN.CO | INFO@EGEN.CO | 717.461.3436

eGenCo

Generation Culture Transformation
Specializing in publishing for generation culture change

Visit us Online at:
www.egen.co

Write to: eGenCo
824 Tallow Hill Road
Chambersburg, PA 17202 USA
Phone: 717-461-3436
Email: info@egen.co

facebook.com/egenbooks

youtube.com/egenpub

egen.co/blog